The Million Dollar Dog Brand

An Entrepreneur's Essential Guide to Creating Demand, Profit & Influence

By: J. Nichole Smith

DESERT ISLAND
PRESS

For Media Inquiries with Nichole, please contact: **hello@workingwithdog.com**

A catalogue record of this book is available from the British Library.

ISBN 978-0-9957841-0-9 (print)
ISBN 978-0-9957841-1-6 (ebk)

Author Photo: Nicholas Dawkes
Cover Design: Knezevic Nevena
Book Editing: Catherine Traffis

For every brave soul who looked at their dog and thought, 'All I want to do is spend all my time with you' and then braved the fear, the self-doubt and the critics to chase a life where that became possible. I know how hard it is. You are my heroes. Every single one of you.

This book is for you.

Table of Contents

Acknowledgments ... 6

1. Foreword ... 9

2. Getting Started ... 12

3. Becoming the Purple Dog ... 19

4. Two Paths to Standing Out ... 22

5. Million Dollar Dog Brand ... 29

6. Million Dollar Dog Brand Formula ... 38

7. Dogly Principles ... 40

8. The Big Marketing Picture ... 46

9. Two Routes to Revenue ... 49

10. What is Marketing? ... 53

11. Six Stages of Marketing ... 59

12. Six Marketing Senses ... 68

13. Sense One ... 73

14. Sense Two ... 132

15 Sense Three ... 154

16. Sense Four 166

17. Sense Five ... 208

18. Sense Six 229

19. Conclusion ... 248

20. Afterward ... 250

21. About the Author ... 254

Acknowledgements

A book is a heavy thing. In a lot of ways, it feels a lot bigger than it actually is. I mean, it's simply words on pages, after all, right? Wrong. The making of a book is a lot like building a brand, it's alchemy. It's method and it's magic. It's solitary, and it takes a village.

For this book to be possible, it feels like an impossible number of wonderful people had to say yes. Firstly, to the inspiring, ridiculously hard-working Million Dollar Dog Brand founders featured in this book, thank you for saying yes to this conversation.

Many of you didn't know me when I tapped you on the shoulder and you gave the most generous gift anyone can offer... your valuable time. This book is possible because you were willing to contribute. Thank you Matt, Will, Steph, Lucy, Vic, Thadeu, Lorien, Carol and Patrick. Thank you for being open enough to help the next generation of petpreneurs learn from your example.

Although they might not know it, my Bootcampers and the Founding Members of Working with Dog are at least 50% of the reason this book exists. When I launched workingwithdog.com in February of 2016 I promised you a free copy of this book. Although I hadn't written it yet, I knew I had to keep my promise. Thank you for believing in me, in this process, for joining me on the journey and for unknowingly giving me accountability. I am so awed by the mountains each and every one of you is moving, one inch at a time, and it's an honor to be near to celebrate your wins and transformations with you.

To my partners in business and branding, John and Gila Kurtz, who shared their little idea with me in 2005 and who have worked tirelessly to ensure its continued growth and success, thank you.

Partnerships are hard and entrepreneurship is gruelling but you two remain remarkable doers. No excuses, just grit. Although my path led me 5,000 miles in another direction, I am incredibly grateful for the devotion you've shown to Dog is Good. It's a great source of pride for me that our baby has grown up so nicely and that's down to your exceptional combined endurance.

Thank you to the various members of my global team who have contributed immensely to making this book possible. To Tracey for being my wordpress superhero and making workingwithdog.com happen at all. To Antonia for lending me some of your genius and radiance. To Sahra for cheerfully doing so many of the brutal tasks required to make this thing real (#transcriptions). To Amanda for being the reason I was ever brave enough to start down this path in the first place and for letting me hold on while you went first. To Claire for helping me find focus and strength to let go. To Jamie for making introductions and being a fierce and wonderful industry ally and friend. To Niall for being my constant companion in digital scheming and for making my nit-picky designs come to life.

To the rest of my friends and family who are the best cheerleaders anyone could ask for. Thank you for your uplifting messages and home-cooked meals, for letting me use your homes as an office, for flying across the world to see me, for trips to the beach, and for understanding when I'm all skyped-out! I know I don't say it enough, but you make my world warm, soft, vibrant and real. Even for those of us separated by great distances, knowing the next time I see you will be like no time has passed at all makes me feel supremely lucky and loved. For you, trouble twins, I know our next adventure isn't far off and I can't wait to discover what it will be! Finally, to my husband, Phil. The reason I wake up every day and pinch myself because I can't believe this life is mine. Thank you for your uncompromising support, your brilliant mind, your steady example and your ability to turn any situation into a game full of laughter and beautiful possibilities. You are one in a million and I am so infatuated with each and every day we have together, to spend walking the dog, cooking fajitas, watching Netflix, drinking beers in the sun and building brands.

xx Nic

1. Foreword

"The hairs on the back of my neck stood up for an instant, and I felt a little sick, a little dizzy. I felt like I was looking over a precipice at something beautiful and mesmerizing, but dangerous. I'd experienced these symptoms before, so I knew immediately what was going on. Such intense emotional and physiological reaction doesn't strike me often, but it happens enough (and consistently enough with the symptoms reported by people all over the world, all throughout history) that I believe I can confidently call it by its name: inspiration. This is what it feels like when an idea comes to you." – Elizabeth Gilbert, Big Magic

"I just knew it, and I remember watching the television and I was shaking all over, I cannot describe to you what it felt like. I literally started shaking, I started just going, "Oh my god that's it, that's it, that's how I'm going to get information out to people. That's it, it's gonna work." - Victoria Stilwell, It's Me or the Dog

It might have been like lightning. The soft little hairs on your neck standing up, sickly stomach, shaking hands, the racing heart that pushes you nervously and urgently forward. It might have been a vague notion, a nagging little question, a name, or product that just wouldn't leave you alone. It might have evolved organically... you started making the thing or lending your time to the thing and it blossomed into a real chance – a living, breathing business. Maybe you didn't choose it; it chose you.

Perhaps it hasn't been to visit you yet – your idea – and you're still waiting for that special something to catch your fancy and woo you away from your current path.

Or maybe you've been working hard for what feels like most of your life and you're just ready to shift to something that feels a lot more like passion and lot less like drudgery.

The fact is, it doesn't matter how it happened, or if it's happened. It doesn't matter where you are in your journey, or how long you've been dreaming or doing. It doesn't matter your age, race, gender, lifestyle, location, or credit score... and really, it doesn't even matter if you like dogs or want to start a pet-related brand! For you, dear reader, all that matters, is that you're genuinely curious about the secrets of building a business that is wildly profitable, popular, and influential and you're willing to join me on this adventure with an open mind and a willing spirit.

Buyer Beware.

Like an exercise you haven't done in a while, entrepreneurship makes you sore in places you didn't know you had. Eventually, after the honeymoon period wears off (three days or three years) a critical moment comes... A moment when you must face up to one inalienable fact: running a business is bloody hard work! The original sun-soaked dream you had about this breezy self-employed lifestyle might feel like just mirage and the initial idea you chased may not be enough to drag you through the tough times. But with any luck, this book will be.

Don't just build a business. Build a brand.

In this book, I will share with you an exact roadmap for building a successful brand – a brand that profits. A brand that has waiting lists and mega-fans and makes a positive difference. A brand that you're proud to be associated with.

A brand that gives you choices: How will you craft your ideal lifestyle? How many millions will you accept from investors? How will you build a culture that attracts top talent? How will you change the world?

The best part of all of this is that you don't need to be famous or have unending amounts of free time; you don't need to have special connections or a fancy degree; you don't need to be independently wealthy, look like a supermodel or even have past experience in branding, business, or whatever it is you intend to sell. All you need is this book, a hefty dose of grit and determination, and the willingness to push past your preconceived notions, your limitations and the naysayers who aren't brave enough to do what you're doing. All that, and a willingness to make to start.

2. Getting Started

"Over the years I've had a lot of ideas, I think like everyone has many, many ideas of something that's missing in the world that they'd like to see. The ideas I've acted on are the ones that I couldn't forget. I couldn't shake. I would try to move on and just keep living the life I was living. This was especially true with BarkBox. Believe it or not, I really, really didn't want to do this business. Life was going really well, I had a very good, easy job, didn't have to work too hard, was paid really well. These are good things. My wife also really didn't want me to do this. But I couldn't help it. I just couldn't help it... that's how you know it's the right idea. It drags you in, and you just start doing it. It's not even really a choice." -Matt Meeker, Co-founder, BarkBox

Most successful entrepreneurs would agree that there is no substitute for just starting. "Learn by doing" we love to say... "start before it's perfect," "start before you're ready," just start!

This advice is sound. It's the truest, best advice there is for anyone just starting out. However, it's probably the last thing you want to hear because starting is so much scarier than chilling in the sublime safety of tasks like buying domain names or obsessing over the details of your widget. But I want to start this book as I mean to continue, by keeping it real.

First and foremost, I want to make it very clear that putting time, energy, and resources towards building a brand is NOT an excuse to delay starting. Reading and working through this book can be done simultaneously with the critical work that your business requires. As you'll discover in these pages, many of the Million Dollar Dog Brands we feature did NOT have it all figured out when they began – they just followed their gut into the realization of an idea. They didn't let the nuances of the perfect color palette or lack of budget for a logo get in the way.

There will be an uncomfortable middle ground where you feel you don't have all the answers. You're going to want to wait until you do to start. Don't wait. Do what you can do now without the answers. Stepping bravely into the unknown is the signature move of an entrepreneur. Like it or not, this is something you're gonna have to get used to. It's terrifying. It can create messes for later. It's not perfect. Deal with it and just start.

If you've already got a business, working through this book and putting resources toward building a brand are NOT a means to avoid doing the work of building a business, selling the product, talking to your customers, or shipping units out the door. Does building a great brand lead to success, profit, and freedom? Yes. Will it happen all by itself without the other boring business slog?

Absolutely not.

As you're building your Million Dollar Dog Brand you may have a somewhat awkward period where you're really excited about the new while still supporting the old. My advice is to keep operating as-is until the Million Dollar Dog Brand is built and unveiled. Don't rush it. This is a natural part of the process and it's very important you keep your momentum up. It won't be awkward forever.

You're Not Alone

"When I started, I had this sort of really rudimentary business plan that specified how many containers of the food I needed to sell in a week to break even. Basically, when I got the website set up I went in and placed a pretend order and then logged into PayPal to make sure it had all gone through successfully and there was actually an order in there from a lady in Virginia. So, that was pretty shocking! I really wasn't ready for it. I didn't have a FedEx or a UPS account or anything set up. I got the inventory, which was being stored on a pallet in my garage, I got some bubble wrap, boxed it up for her and then drove down to the UPS Store and I think I spent something like $40 to overnight her this box of food that she paid $8 shipping for. I went home and scratched my head and said, 'I need to get this part of it figured out.' I hadn't really thought that bit through yet because I actually wasn't expecting orders so soon."

– Lucy, Honest Kitchen

"Neither one of us have our MBAs, but we sort of felt like we were great consumers, that we knew brands, we knew design, we knew what we liked, we felt like we had a good eye for things, and we knew we had a great story to tell. So, we decided we wanted to tell that to the end consumer through a catalogue and through a website and we also wanted to tell that story to retailers to help them tell it to the end consumer, so we started all of that simultaneously. We did everything on our own, quite locally and very slowly, and very... is rustically a word? Very old-school! Very grassroots, but it was great, it worked." - Stephanie, Planet Dog

"It wasn't really until I came over to Manhattan that I decided to set up my own dog training business. By then, I felt I had enough experience to put myself out there. Manhattan is a difficult place in and of itself, setting business up there, dealing with all the different kinds of people, let alone the dogs, I mean the dogs are the easy thing! That was a baptism by fire for me, but I really believed the two years I spent with Dog Trainers in New York (which was my company that I set up with another trainer) were the best years for learning, because I was thrown in the deep end, and I learned so much." – Victoria Stilwell

Mindset Moment: "I'm Not Ready"

What are the stories you're telling yourself about why now isn't the right time, about why you are not worthy or ready, and what you believe (consciously or unconsciously) needs to occur before you're "allowed" to have "it" – whatever it may be. Do you need more money? More time? Do you need to be skinnier, more qualified, or more confident? Do you need to be happier, sleep better, or have less on your plate?

Spoiler alert: You are not going to wake up one day and feel ready. Ever. This time will never come. Here is the harsh reality: people all over the world have done it, AND ARE DOING IT RIGHT NOW with less time, fewer resources, and fewer advantages than you. Are you just going to let them leave you in the dust?

There is no award for waiting until you feel ready, but there are a lot of consequences, including missing out entirely and wondering for the rest of your life what might have been.

"Why would you let fear hold you back? If you don't apply to Harvard you won't get in. That's always been my mantra. Why can't you? Why couldn't I do it? When I pitched It's Me or the Dog, nobody knew who I was; I was just a trainer. But I had the right idea at the right time and it hit, it stuck. But it never would have happened if I didn't try to make it happen. I also believe ideas with passion behind them are so much more likely to take off"
– Victoria Stilwell

Waiting for the right time is just fear dressed up as good sense. Yesterday was the right time to start, but today will do just fine. So, repeat after me:

> **"I have everything I need to be successful.**
> **I don't need to wait anymore."**

If this makes you uncomfortable, I want you to (right now) write that mantra on a post-it note and put it on your mirror, computer, or fridge; somewhere you'll see it every day... and also set a daily alarm on your phone with this message. Say it out loud when you see it. Rinse and repeat until you believe it.

The Brand Is Not the Cake

Remember, your brand is the icing, sprinkles, awesome shop, friendly staff, cute packaging and fun signage that makes the customer buy the cake, buy it again, Instagram the hell out of it, share it with friends, and pay twice as much for your cake over the other guys." The brand is not the cake. Is it just as essential if you want to run a successful bakery? Yes! But don't ignore the cake. Ok? (Excuse me, I'll be right back, I need to make tea and eat some cake!)

Building a brand is what businesses do to stand out. To be difficult to compete with. To make more money. To build demand and influence. To have more fun. Building a brand is what entrepreneurs do to escape being owned by the drudgery of a business, in order to embrace being the leader of a movement, the curator of a fashion, the instigator of a revolution, the designer of a lifestyle, and an architect of their own freedom.

Building a dog brand is about doing all of that within the pet industry, which at the time of writing this book, is an industry that just surpassed $100 billion in value worldwide.[1] The marketplace is crowded. The space is noisy. Everyone and their dog (literally) wants a piece of this cake!

So what does that mean for you? There is only one way you're going to build a sustainable future as a player in the pet industry. The time for fitting in is over; you have got to stand out.

---

1 http://www.petfoodindustry.com/blogs/7-adventures-in-pet-food/post/6263-global-pet-care-sales-pass-100-billion-for-first-time

"In a crowded marketplace, fitting in is failing."

-Seth Godin, The Purple Cow

3. Becoming the Purple Dog

In his book Purple Cow, Seth Godin proposes that it simply is not enough to make a basically acceptable product and then hire people to market and sell it for you. This was the way it worked in the "good old days" (which he calls the "TV Industrial Age") but in our crazy 24/7 media-filled world and in the highly-saturated pet industry, the only strategy that works is to stand out. To be remarkable. To be a purple cow in a field of black-and-white Holsteins. Or for our purposes, a purple dog.

This is counterintuitive. It goes against our programming. Humans want to fit in because it's how we find the belonging we crave. We learn as pups that it is safer to do what we're told. To dress, talk, and act like everyone else. We learn early on that the most mortifying thing we could ever be is embarrassed. We perfect the art of "normal" and we can usually avoid negative attention... we can usually avoid any attention at all. Most of us are predisposed to camouflage ourselves, to disappear into the masses. To learn the winning social formula for acceptance and then copy it like a human chameleon.

"You can't assume what everybody else is doing is working, or that the same thing is best for you because it might be working for a huge company. You'll get lost if you try to look like them."
– Lorien, PetHub

The logic of "just be normal" makes it easy to see the appeal of copying other people's good ideas. I mean hey, if you can offer basically the same thing someone else has already built demand for, but undercut the price of the original, or make it easier to acquire, you can build a very viable business.
We all know there are plenty of people out there who are happy to pay less and buy the knockoff version of a branded product. I mean, let's be honest, most of us are happy saving a couple of bucks to buy the generic version of something; especially if that something is low stakes for our reputation like beans, breakfast cereal, or detergent. But even if we buy them, most of us are not interested in creating and selling copycat products. It just doesn't satisfy our values, or our ego.

"There are many, many, many people who have amazing ideas. All over the place, all over the world and there is room for everybody in any industry in any market. I truly believe that. You have to be innovative, you know? I think it's so easy to sort of just jump on a bandwagon because it's happening and it's easy, but I think if you're a true entrepreneur and you have a really good idea... make it stand out! Be innovative. That's what's going to catch the attention. Create your own bandwagon." - Stephanie, Planet Dog

If you are happy to settle for being just another "me too," please exit stage left. Stop reading. Go away and get inspired in your own life and passion and come back when you're ready to do the work. I am not interested in helping you profit off someone else's blood, sweat, and tears. Plus, there are WAY easier ways to make money ... go read The 4-Hour Work Week find something you can sell and automate and go make your uninspired fortune.

For the rest of us, if you're still reading this, you likely have a deep urge to be a maker. To create. To bring to life something remarkable... to not only create wealth, but to do work that satisfies and fulfils you and maybe change the world in the process. Is this you? Then you're in the right place. Pay attention, here comes your roadmap.

4. Two Paths to Standing Out

Opportunity has often been described as "finding the gap" in the market and filling it. As makers, this often begins when we set out to make "the same thing but better." In most cases, it is a small tweak or series of improvements that makes something that already exists better. This is your first opportunity to avoid disappearing into the noise: Create a sensational product.

Sometimes, we don't have a thing, but we know what we believe in; we know what we admire. Sometimes it's the stories, the design, the beauty, and the platform we're passionate about, and the thing is less important. We package it better, describe it differently, apply it in a new way, or for an audience we know how to speak to. This is the core of the second opportunity: Create a sensational brand.

1. Sensational Products

"I think a lot of products or items that are really useful inventions come out of necessity. Somebody in the backcountry, or somebody fiddling with a tool, and realizing there is a better way to do it. Then other people appreciate those efforts and see the benefits and they embrace it." - Patrick, Ruffwear

"When we set out to make dog beds, we went back to the drawing board and said, "What makes the perfect bed?" We looked at every single, tiny aspect of what makes a pet bed great. It may sound silly, it's a cushion after all, but we identified six specific elements to the perfect dog bed: design, quality, durability, practicality, eco-friendliness, and social responsibility. Even in the higher-end segment, most companies focus on one or two, at most three of those six things, but very rarely do you see a company take holistic approach to create a very well-balanced product. That's what we set out to do." -Will, P.L.A.Y.

Some of you reading this right now don't have an eye toward building an empire. You might even find the title of this book a little awkward because you're not even sure you're that interested in building a brand – you just want to make some great "thing." Maybe there's a problem you're passionate about solving, or an audience or a cause you're invested in serving, and you're dedicated to doing it better than it's already been done. Maybe you're not sure why; maybe an idea just floated in through your window and landed in your notebook and you can't shake it.

Or maybe the thing you do simply for the pure pleasure of it has turned out to be something people want, need, and are willing to pay for, and everyone is urging you to make and sell this thing. Sometimes there is just something you HAVE to do and you don't know why. You don't have a plan for greatness; you're simply dedicated to the problem, the craft, or the cause.

Many of the world's greatest dog brands were born this way: Ruffwear started because of a guy's obsession with making the perfect, lightweight, waterproof dog water bowl for the trail. P.L.A.Y. was founded because a pug puppy kept peeing on or destroying every dog bed her doting parents bought for her, so they set out to make one she would approve of.

Honest Kitchen began because of a gal's obsession with healing her dog's chronic ear infections through the power of wholesome nutrition.

Harry Barker was born when it's founder fell deathly ill and to keep herself busy, she started making chic dog beds to match her friends' fashionable New York apartments.

The difference between Ruffwear, Honest Kitchen, and Harry Barker and all the thousands of other pet product startups we've never heard of, is that these products stood out in the crowd. These products caught the attention of influential people because they were different in some way. Most importantly, different in a way that was immediately noticeable, no explanation required. These petpreneurs did not start out to create huge brands or make millions of dollars; they simply had a desire to make something special – to provide something for their own dogs or their friends' dogs that improved their quality of life.

These pioneering pet businesses didn't consider the cost, the return on investment, the market potential, or the five-year plan when they made that first thing – they simply sat down, learned about their craft and made the best thing they could. Then they improved it and improved it until they were pleased enough with the result to share it. Sensational products don't fit in because they were built with love, passion, and a total dedication to achieving a desired result.

2. Sensational Brands

"I would not call Alex or myself marketing experts, but I think we are very good branders and that's where our expertise comes in. Alex is brilliant. He has just this amazing brilliant mind and he's an amazing designer and we have another amazing designer that we have been working with since day one. She essentially helped us create this brand and she can see the bigger picture. She can see what we wanted to try to achieve, which is a very colorful, innovative, fun look that people will be drawn to for their dogs." - Stephanie, Planet Dog

"Why couldn't your dog leash be an extension of your lifestyle just like the shoes you're wearing, or the purse, or the watch? It could be and it should be an extension of your personal style. If I'm going out and I'm all in black and I want my dog leash to be black as well, and if my girlfriend is wearing leopard shoes, maybe her dog leash should have the leopard print too. So I think with that mentality, we ended up hitting the sweet spot in the global niche and that's one of the reasons why we grew so quickly, not just in Brazil. Because every dog owner in the world felt the necessity of having cool pet products." -Thad, Zee.Dog

Some of you reading this book were born with the powerful desire to bring something epic and beautiful to the world. You might be fuzzy on the details, but you're clear on one thing: You want to build an empire. You see opportunity everywhere and you know you have the skills to build something remarkable. You feel that there is something bigger than you, urging you forward. Oftentimes you can't quite name or explain what it is that you're meant for, but you know it's not your fate to sit quietly in the corner.
You might be a "serial entrepreneur" or you might be waiting to find "your thing" – you are poised and ready to leap into action when you can wrap your mind around what exactly it is you're meant to be doing, find an opportunity you can't ignore, or the essential message you are passionate about spreading.

Many sensational dog brands are born this way: through the sheer will and resolve of visionary dreamers or doers.

At a time when most "dog themed" stuff was a bit cheesy and cartoony, my partners John and Gila Kurtz and I had a vision to create something tangible that showed off our love of dogs but were also sophisticated and clever. We knew whatever it was needed to be design and message-led. First and foremost, we knew who our audience was, and the rest would follow... Dog is Good was born.

Tom Arnold left Microsoft, happy to leave the corporate machine for the life an entrepreneur, but not sure how to use his tech skills to help the love of his life: his dog. In his search for inspiration he stumbled onto these heart-breaking statistics: Only 25% of dogs and only 2% of cats that are lost and find their way into shelters make it back home to their owners. He knew his mission was to use technology to help lost pets get home: PetHub and the digital ID tag was born.

Matt Meeker was repeatedly disappointed with the ability of his local pet stores in New York to suggest new treats and toys for him to bring home to his Great Dane, Hugo. Consequently, he became consumed with the idea of finding personalized ways to help dog parents delight their dogs on a regular basis. Thus, BarkBox was born.
Stephanie Volo was chatting her buddies about what environmentally friendly thing they could make and sell to make a difference in the world, when they looked at the dogs sleeping at their feet and inspiration struck. Planet Dog was born.

Thadeu Diz adopted a dog and discovered that there simply wasn't a pet accessory brand cool enough for him to connect with. Inspiration gripped him and he knew that he had to build a brand for Pet Parents like him. Zee.Dog was born.

Victoria Stilwell discovered early in her career as a dog trainer just how little most people understand about dogs and their behavior. She became obsessed with reaching as many people as possible as quickly as possible to help educate and empower humans to learn about their canine companions and treat them with the respect they deserve. It's Me or the Dog and Victoria Stilwell Positively were born.

Petpreneurs like myself, John and Gila, Will and Deb, Tom, Matt, Stephanie, Thad and Victoria invested heavily in one simple idea and have worked tirelessly to pursue that vision. The inspiration and the audience were clear from the beginning, and though the products and services may change over time, the mission will remain. These sensational brands don't fit in because the leaders behind them are selling a feeling, a lifestyle, or a message. They have built an engaged audience around that feeling or message and everything they do is in the singular aim of spreading it with everyone they encounter.

Ruffwear, P.L.A.Y, Honest Kitchen, Harry Barker, Dog is Good, PetHub, BarkBox, Planet Dog, Zee.Dog, Planet Dog and Victoria Stilwell... all of these guys and gals are purple dogs. They stand out in a sea of black and white spots. They are impossible to ignore. **They are Million Dollar Dog Brands.**

5. Million Dollar Brand

A Million Dollar Brand is the ultimate purple dog: a sensational brand that sells sensational products. It is the perfect formula for standing out. These brands have it all: the looks and the smarts, the form and the function. In this case, the words "million dollar" are less about literally being worth a million dollars, and much more about the intrinsic "pricelessness" of a valuable brand. You may never earn a million dollars, or earn 20 million and still be a "Million Dollar Dog Brand." The term is symbolic; a description of the type of business you are... the type of business that focuses both on offering a sensational product AND on building a sensational brand. You can be a groomer, a dog walker, a pet product manufacturer, an online retailer, a pet psychic – it doesn't matter what you do or how much you earn – what matters is your dedication and attention to both your superior product/service and your brand. Most of the value of Million Dollar Brands lies in the almost impossible-to-quantify brand value – which is made up of a messy mix of the actual, tangible quality of the product or service, and the pricelessness of the "know, like, and trust" the brand has earned from its audience.

Why Should I Build a Million Dollar Brand?

If a brand is worth its weight in gold, a Million Dollar Dog Brand is worth its weight in diamonds. As you'll read in the stories throughout this book, it almost appears as if success just happens by accident for Million Dollar Dog Brands.

Obviously, there is a lot of hard work and unseen toil that goes on in the background to achieve these wins, but MDDBs do have some decided advantages that create this illusion of overnight success. Based on our research, we've summed these major brand advantages up into a three-part cycle.

Million Dollar Dog Brand Advantage Cycle

1. **POPULARITY**: Attract word of mouth and free buzz

2. **PROFIT**: Additional demand leads to higher profits

3. **POWER**: Social change and industry disruption

1. POPULARITY: Buzz

"I had an editor call me one day from Outside Magazine, and keep in mind, I'm working out of my garage. I've got three businesses going out of my garage. A crew showing up in the morning to get boat cleaning supplies, for my marine business. I've got faxes that are ringing calling at 3 am from Japan, ordering products for my Paddle Gear business. In all of this, I'm packing boxes and putting header cards on Ruffwear gear, and getting it out the door and the phone rings, and I run in and grab it and Bob Howls is on the phone. Bob says, "Hey, I'd like to include some of your product in the book. I was wondering if you could send me some samples." And I said, "Well yeah, sure! I can send them out. What color do you want?" and Bob goes, "Well I don't know. What color would you suggest?" And I went, "Well, if you're going to put it in a publication, I would probably choose red, it looks pretty good in red." He goes, "Okay, why don't you send me a couple of those?" And I said, "Okay, sounds great." And I'm writing down his information and I said, "How do you want to pay for these?" And there was a long pause... He said, "Well, I don't think you want to make me pay for these." I said, "Well Bob, I can't keep doing this. I'm sending them out the door. People are asking for these things...

It's crazy." And you know, keep in mind, I'm running in and out, trying to fill out the UPS forms, with carbon forms, carbon paper to get all this done. And Bob says, "Well, let me just tell you, I'm going to put this in the 12 perfect presents for the holiday gift buying guide and it's going to be worth about $50,000 to $70,000 in advertising to you." And I said, "Okay yeah, that sounds good. I'll send them out." – Patrick, Ruffwear

"I was very lucky that I got a couple of cool bits of PR coverage. I had sent a press release out, just sort of announcing the existence of the company and explaining what the food was, and it got picked up in a couple of dog magazines and then really it was just the word of mouth..." – Lucy, Honest Kitchen

"An editor saw the bed in somebody's loft and said, "Oh that's so pretty, let's photograph it for InStyle!" They borrowed the bed and I made a couple more and then next thing you know we're selling them from editorial exposure. I didn't know it was a million-dollar idea, but then people started calling and we got more press and people would call my home phone number because I didn't know you shouldn't put your home phone number in a national magazine. And then Bloomingdales called and wanted to buy 500 dog beds." - Carol, Harry Barker

Million Dollar Brands are purple dogs, so they stand out. MDDBs get more attention, not just from consumers but from the media as well. Million Dollar Dog Brands get more free press so they get a free boost to their marketing efforts. Because of this natural boost, there is more demand for MDDB products and services. Additionally, consumers are attracted to purple dogs and excited to talk about them so the powerful, positive impact of word-of-mouth comes into effect quickly and exponentially for MDDBs.

Since there is a direct correlation between referrals and purchase, word of mouth is largely regarded as the most effective form of marketing so Buzz, this first advantage, is quite a significant one.

2. PROFIT: Demand

"The first month was us carrying around an image on our phone and showing people and saying "What do you think about this idea?" People would get excited about it and say, "That's really great, let me know when it's live and I'll buy it." After a few of those interactions I started to carry a Square and I would just plug it into my phone and say, "It's live, swipe your card," just taking orders in person. That was our first fifty or so orders. We happened to put it live in mid-November, which is a good time because we were going into the holiday season, and obviously, that's a time of year when people buy. Initially we didn't know how big the audience might be, and we were okay if it were 100 people. It turns out it's a lot larger than that; now we have about a quarter-million subscribers."
- Matt, BarkBox

"Before too long, a friend of mine from the dog park who had a local pet supply store wanted to carry the food and so I kind of set up wholesale pricing and sent some to her. She sold through it unbelievably quickly, and then a few other stores wanted to carry it because consumers had asked them, "You know I've been feeding this to my dog, it's really cool, would you consider carrying it?" And then stores would call me, and then once we had a critical mass of stores, then distributors started to calling and said, "Hey, you know, our reps have been in some stores and have seen your product, would you consider selling it to us?" Within a couple of years of starting the business, I actually ended up having my first daughter, and so we quickly thought we better add a member of staff to try and help because it was hard keeping her and the desk and trying to do all the emails during the day.

In terms of the growth, it did kind of take-off surprisingly quickly. It was incredible. The night before I had my daughter, I think we packed up 39 boxes of food to ship out to customers, which seems small now but it was pretty overwhelming at the time." - Lucy, Honest Kitchen

The second stage of the MDDB advantage cycle is where revenue begins to grow. Because of the increase in demand for the products or services of a Million Dollar Dog Brand, they often have waiting lists, can charge more, and generally don't suffer from "not enoughness." Their problems are much more about how to increase their capacity and create infrastructure to keep up with demand. Overall, this leads to a more profitable company. Because they often don't need cash to survive, but to scale, investors are usually very interested too.

3. POWER: Influence

"A big part of the company has always been that we want to make all dogs happy... That's not just the dogs that are in good homes and can afford to buy BarkBox. It's also the dogs that need a good home or need a better home. When we started we said, "We're really committed to this, and we'll donate to rescues and shelters and that'll help." And that all helps. But it feels like there's a lot of donation in the rescue world, which is needed, but it's not changing the curve of that problem fast enough for our impatience. So, while we're committed to still donating, we also want to build products and solutions in addition to just donating money. BarkBuddy is an attempt of that, taking a really fun, mobile experience, that seems to work in the dating world and applying it to discover your new rescue dog, or discover your new dog that you can rescue. We've since brought the product even further, where people can connect with the rescue and almost order the dog directly. It still has a long way to go, and it's only one attempt of many technology solutions we're working on in that area. I have this kind of silly personal dream of having a ranch somewhere where we host a lot of dogs and help them get the best homes, but I think if over time we build up a whole network and stable of solutions, we can really make a bigger dent in the problem." - Matt, BarkBox

"In 2006 we created the Planet Dog Foundation to support non-profits across the country whose focus is training, placing, and supporting any sort of dog working to give people independence, to save their lives, or to enhance their lives in one way or another: a therapy dog, a service dog, a search and rescue dog – any sort of dog that works to help a person in need. That's when we decided to give 2% of our sales to the foundation so that we could really make an impact. So, that's 2% of our sales, not 2% of our profit. We've given about a million and a half away since 2006." – Stephanie, Planet Dog

"From the very beginning I remember my husband saying, "I want us to teach people," I mean we could teach them on TV but we wanted to teach people to be trainers. That's what we're doing now. It's one thing to have courses or seminars – but to actually set up an academy where people are going to come and they're going to learn how to be dog trainers is a whole different deal, it's massive. But the problem we still have, especially in the United States, but also in a lot of other different countries, is that there are still so many trainers out there training old-school, traditional styles that concentrate more on punishing dogs and forcing dogs to obey. While our academy is going to be churning out trainers that follow modern behavioral and cognitive science. These guys are going to be educated with the latest research, they're going to be taught how to do things in the right way. It's top of the line. These guys are going to help change the lives of dogs positively. These guys are going to change the world." - Victoria Stilwell

The next stage in the cycle is power. Due to being an "always in the news" brand and having cash to play with, the Million Dollar Dog Brand earns incredible influence and can choose to grow in ways that benefit its employees, communities, and the planet. This influence equates to power to create social change, the power to disrupt entire industries, and the power to support and educate entire populations. Million Dollar Dog Brands can bring significant attention and cash to causes they care about. Million Dollar Dog Brands have a chance to change the world... but it is the first two stages of the cycle that allow the brand to achieve this level of impact.

When you are entrepreneur and your business has buzz, demand, and influence – the advantages spread far beyond your business and seep into your life. Opportunities pop up that you may never have dreamed of: exotic trips, five-figure checks for speaking gigs, franchising, licensing, the ability to push forward causes you care about – and freedom of choice. Growth does not have to equal overwhelm. When you're not desperate to pay the bills, you can make decisions for the right reasons. You can craft your life in the way you desire. You can create an empire and become an authority or you can simply create a job you love that affords you the lifestyle you want. Owning a Million Dollar Brand means the choice is yours.

Sustainable Competitive Advantage

"We literally were the first ones on the market. We essentially paved the way for some of our competitors... they watched what we were doing and then they tried to replicate it. The good news for us is that none of them have replicated the comprehensiveness with which we have approached this because we're not looking to make a buck on QR tags for dogs, we've created a brand that's gonna get as many lost pets home as quickly as possible and keep them out of shelters." - Lorien, PetHub

The sum of buzz, demand, and influence is the holy grail of
business goals: a sustainable competitive advantage. "Competitive
advantage" meaning you have advantages over your competition;
"Sustainable" meaning you can maintain those advantages over
time. Can you be successful without building a brand? Yes.
Definitely.

For example, if you've invented a unique product and you own a
patent so no one can really duplicate it and you're selling to
businesses who desperately need it, a brand is pretty irrelevant.
You'll be successful because the demand is great and you're the
only supply. But this is a rare business and it all hinges on demand
staying high for that one widget, so you have success but it might
not be sustainable. You are at the mercy of many factors you can't
control.

If you're like most entrepreneurs, you're doing or selling something
that is pretty similar to what your competition is making or selling,
and your options are limited for standing out. Those options
usually include: be the cheapest or build a brand. Being the
cheapest is not sustainable because anyone can undercut you on
price and compete.

Building a brand is sustainable because it's very difficult to compete
with the emotional connection and that people have with the
brands they trust. If you don't really have competition now, don't
worry, you will. When that time comes, you want to have
something more than just product specs or price to lean on.

How Do I Build a Million Dollar Brand?

Brand building is not a science, it's more like alchemy: a slightly mysterious process made up of data, passion, art, and connection (and in most cases a bit of serendipity)! Lucky for you, by mixing up widely accepted marketing theory with the successful techniques of those who've gone before, we have created a clear picture of what it takes to become a Million Dollar Dog Brand.

This book will give you a roadmap. A step-by-step path: **A Million Dollar Brand formula.**

6. Million Dollar Dog Brand Formula

This book is all about giving you an exact roadmap to create your own Million Dollar Dog Brand. It doesn't matter where you're at right now... you may have a business already and you're looking to refresh or kickstart what you've already got, or you may be dreaming up a new business that you're committed to giving its best chance. No matter what, this book will be an indispensable guide to help you navigate the rocky climb up Million Dollar Dog Brand Mountain. My suggestion is that you read this book all the way through once, and then read it again, doing the exercises one at a time along the way.

What to Expect

Before we dive in to the Million Dollar Dog Brand Formula we are going to go over a few concepts to provide a bit of context:

1. The Dogly Principles
2. The Big Picture
3. Your Two Routes to Revenue
4. What Is Marketing and Why Does It Matter
5. The Six Stages of Marketing
6. Where Will Your Brand Fit In

Once we've gotten clear on why your brand matters, we will break your Million Dollar Dog Brand roadmap down into six primary steps: Why, Who, What, Where and How (Part 1 and Part 2). To make it as easy as possible to follow, each of the six steps will be broken down into four sections:

1. What is it?
2. Why does it matter?
3. How does it show up?
4. How can it be mastered?

Each of these sections will be broken down into practical and actionable steps. Along the way, we've offered plenty of resources and tools to assist you, so keep that highlighter or notepad nearby! Plus, in each section we'll add in some real-world stories from the 10 Million Dollar Dog Brands that we interviewed for the book. Those brands include (in no particular order):

Million Dollar Dog Brands

1. Dog is Good
2. BarkBox
3. Ruffwear
4. Planet Dog
5. Harry Barker
6. P.L.A.Y.
7. PetHub
8. Victoria Stilwell
9. Zee.Dog
10. Honest Kitchen

At the very end, you can learn a little bit more about me and where to find me or get in touch if you so desire.

7. The 5 Dogly Principles

Before you start down the road, I want to give you some rules to live by. Throughout more than a decade of experience as a photographer, an entrepreneur, a consultant, a grad student, and most recently through my research for this book, a few basic universal truths have slowly risen to the surface. For years before I had named them, I was striving to achieve these principles. Chances are, you are too! These are the fundamental principles of what I believe it is to be a good person, a good business, a good boss, and a brilliant brand.

I sometimes call these principles "the five secrets to small business success," not as a gimmick, but because I genuinely believe these "secrets" are the five essential principles to not only survive, but thrive in your business. They are "secrets" not because they've never been written about, discussed or addressed, no... quite the opposite is true. Anywhere you find a great book or speech about succeeding in business, you'll find at least one of these principles lurking. These principles are secrets because they are hidden in plain sight. Because we already know them. Because we're probably already keenly aware of their impact on our audiences, businesses, and lives. But as we all know, what gets measured gets improved. The difference between knowing something and actively implementing it, prioritizing it, and measuring it is vast.
Consider these Dogly Principals your five commandments.

Let them guide the choices, investments, and improvements you make in your business every day. If you're questioning your decisions, don't know how to handle a customer, are getting stuck designing your marketing materials or need some guidelines for training staff, these principles stand at the ready. If all you take from this entire book are these Five Dogly Principles and you're able to stick to them, you'll probably have a pretty successful business and well-loved brand.

1. Generosity
2. Simplicity
3. Authenticity
4. Consistency
5. Quality

1. Generosity

I remember one rainy Seattle day, sitting in my car outside the bank, I was having a long chat with my dad on the phone. I don't recall the exact reason for the conversation, but I remember feeling down and generally frustrated. He said something then that has stuck with me ever since and that I try to implement when I am Grump-a-saurus Rex... and that is "to serve." He said, "If you're feeling angry, frustrated, unloved, or like life isn't fair – serve the person who is upsetting you. Serve anyone! You'll feel better for it!"

The pure act of serving is its own reward. This may sound trite or cliché, but I can tell you from personal experience, having many, many times heard my dad's words in my head and begrudgingly obeyed them – that it is impossible to be upset when you choose to selflessly serve with no agenda. Of course, this applies in business as well. The added bonus is that in addition to the personal fulfilment you get from giving, there are tangible benefits as well.

Make generous giving a core element in your strategy: your company's culture, your customer service policies, and your marketing plan... and you WILL be rewarded financially. Giving equals receiving. It's just an inescapable, universal truth.

The second part to this principle is to have clear boundaries. Most entrepreneurs I work with have the "generous" bit down; it's the boundaries that need some work! So keep in mind these are two sides of the same coin. It is impossible to truly be generous without identifying and protecting your own needs first.

Being generous is not about giving until you have nothing left or charging so little for your products/services that you can't eat. Being generous is about the extra you give on top. It's very much about letting go of negative energy surrounding feeling taken advantage of so you can give freely. It is a recipe for both profitability and happiness, I assure you!

"I do as much as I can, and when we say no we have a very good reason for saying no, and the reason is my schedule won't allow it. I take my job very seriously. I have been blessed with this platform, and now I'm going to use it for good. That means that I will do as many charity events as I can, give away as many books as I can for charity auctions and things like that. Actually being on a board, I don't too many of those because I don't have enough time. When you're starting out in business, especially in the animal business, and you're an expert in some way, you could spend your whole time doing free work, and then you have no career and you can't pay your mortgage. So, you have to have a balance. When I first started with training clients, they used to call me and tell me about their issues, I would be on the phone with them for an hour even before I first saw them. I realized that, wait a second, no, no, no! That's my time, I need to be paid for my time, and I'm going to give away a little bit on the phone but you need to see me.

So I became again, very controlled I think, with how much information I gave away on the phone because I knew I would be much better in person. I think there are people who get upset if you can't do something, but most people understand, and so I just say "Hey, inquire, inquire, because I might be able to do it." And that's my advice: Be generous but have boundaries because there are some people who will just take advantage." – Victoria Stilwell

2. Simplicity

In words, offerings and design... **Less is always more.**

3. Authenticity

Be genuine. Be honest. Be humble. Be Less business machine and more human friend. We will dig into this particular principle quite a bit in the first steps of our Million Dollar Dog Brand formula, but the key to remember here, and it is clichéd but true, is that people do business with people. The more human you can be, the better. The more you grow, and the more distance you get from your customer, the more important this becomes. A Million Dollar Dog Brand ONLY works if it is based in an authentic belief in something bigger than itself. Something more honorable than projections and dividends that all brand communications shout from the rooftops. Authenticity comes through "walking the talk" and genuinely caring about customers.

"I think a mistake that many companies make, is, let's say hypothetically a guy creates a surf brand... but this guy's never surfed in his life, and he doesn't even know how to stand on a surfboard. It's going to be really hard for him to create a brand or content authentic enough that people will actually believe it and want to be part of it.

In our case, the lifestyle of the brand is our life. I mean, if you follow us, you know, on a daily basis, we'll be in these places and we'll be doing these things. These are pictures of our lifestyle and our friends. It's authentic and I think authenticity in branding is the most important thing when you're trying to get people on board to follow your mission." – Thad, Zee.Dog

4. Consistency

There should be consistency in your messaging and in your actions. Use consistent visual cues (colors, fonts, images, styles) to build brand recognition. If all you do is what you say you're going to do, you'll thrill the hell out of your clients and they will come back for more. Consistency is a key element of marketing and branding so you'll probably hear me mention this a half a dozen more times!

"I think our brand is identifiable because we haven't tried to be something we're not, we haven't changed our look, we haven't really changed. I think our brand translates well on many platforms; our products present really well in a catalogue, in a magazine, or on a website. We made sure that everything we did could translate into all of those different types of channels to keep consistency and build brand recognition." – Stephanie, Planet Dog

5. Quality

This one is pretty self-explanatory. Do and send out your best work. Own up to mistakes. Exceed expectations. Quality is a massive catch-all for a lot of big and small daily choices. It's a habit of excellence. A culture of not settling for less than 100%.

"Quality. This one is obvious: you want a product that is absolutely safe. For us, the huge topic of "quality" is made of up lots of little details like craftsmanship, the stitch count, and using extremely high-grade materials.

There are a lot of features I can keep going on and on about that many consumers might not even notice. We use very expensive zippers so they last, we use solid cotton piping, whereas some products I have seen in the market have piping stuffed with nothing, or with paper. Quality as a company means quality in the small, sometimes unnoticed details." - Will, P.L.A.Y.

For a printable version of the Five Dogly Principles, visit:

www.workingwithdog.com/5-dogly-principles/

- or –

email us at hello@dane-dane.com with your mailing address and we'll send you a Dogly Principles postcard!

8. The Big Marketing Picture

OK, who's ready to get going on their branding journey? The first step is to look at the total landscape of our business and its objectives. Why do you have or want a business? When I ask this question, I usually get answers like this:

- Help people and help dogs
- Hang out with dogs
- Work with your hands
- Be your own boss
- Make a living
- Be a part of something that matters
- Because your parents / friends / peers do
- Freedom to work from home

Any of this sound familiar? I am guessing if you're reading this book, it does! So let me ask a different question. Why does a business exist? I am sure you know the answer to this...

The only reason a business exists is to earn revenue.

That's it. No nuance, no "buts" or "ifs" - if you want to run a business, you are signing up to want to make money from that business. If you have no desire to spend a significant percentage of your time managing revenue creation, then my friend, you have an expensive, time-consuming hobby or a charity, not a business. By definition, a business's sole aim is to generate revenue (and ideally, eventually profit).

Do not fall into the common petpreneur trap of believing that because you care deeply about what you do that you can't or shouldn't get paid well to do it. A business is not an emotional entity built up on all your hopes and expectations – inextricably linked to your self-worth, your entire future, and all that you hold dear in the world. Your business is not your baby. Let me repeat that:

Your business is not your baby. It is not a living thing.

Your business is a series of transactions. An experiment. You are free at any time to change your mind, to walk away, or sell it to the highest bidder. The first step in building a business is to be brutal about the reality of what that business is, and to not let it get all mixed up with your personal life. You may not believe me now if you're still staring all lovingly into the eyes of your new business and thinking the love affair will never end – but trust me – at some point, you're going to want to slap that business across the face and run out and slam the door, or collapse in a heap crying about why it won't love you back.

Spoiler alert: Your business will never love you back. But like with most other relationships, by creating super clear boundaries about what you give to it, and what you expect it to give back to you, then you're free to generously pour all that love and passion into it without fear.

Now, the flip-side of the revenue coin is that as consumers we want to feel valued. We want the stuff we buy to be of good quality, we want to receive great service, we want to buy into a story. We want to do business with people, not big faceless, robotic conglomerates importing mystery ingredients to cut their costs by .05% or obsessing over that extra 1% in market share no matter the human or canine cost.

The lesson here is to get the balance right between why you exist as a business (revenue), and what drives you as a human (your values). Both are critical to your success if you're going to build a profitable brand. It is critical that we agree early on that in the context we're discussing here, branding is not just about feeding your ego or about making something beautiful for beauty's sake.

In our world, the goal of building a brand is to create a profitable, sustainable business that delivers to you, its owner, the lifestyle you dream of. That lifestyle will come as a result of the Dogly Principles, the MDDB Advantage Cycle and maybe even as a result of selling your brand one day for a nice tidy sum! #lifegoals

9. Two Routes to Revenue

So the next bit of context we need to dive into is the basic question on every business owner's mind: How do I create more revenue? When I ask this to classes of students the usual suspects inevitably comes up, including:

- ○ Website
- ○ Advertise
- ○ Go to events
- ○ Sponsor
- ○ Sales
- ○ New Products
- ○ Direct mail
- ○ Networking
- ○ Blogging
- ○ Etc.

Indeed, these are all truly great ways to lead you down the path to revenue – but these are all tactics. Let's take a step backward again and keep it more big-picture. Let's talk strategy.

There are only two ways to create revenue. If you think of your business as a mountain that receives more revenue the higher up you go, there are only two routes to the top. This might seem impossible at first blush, but stick with me.

The two routes are basically these:

1. More transactions

2. More per transaction

1. More Transactions

If we think about transactions as sales - we can break down this idea of "more transactions" into two camps:
> a. Clients
> b. Products

Quite simply, we can get more transactions from existing clients, or increase the number of transactions with new clients. With our products, we can sell more of our existing products, or we can create new products and sell those. Or we can combine them: Sometimes a great way to attract new clients is to create a new product that they want, need, or would be attracted to. A combination of these strategies, or any one of them individually, is a sure-fire way to increase revenue in our business.

2. More Per Transaction

The next place to look for revenue growth is the value of each transaction. How much are we earning for every sale? We can increase this number by moving one or both of these two levers:
> a. Volume
> b. Value

In this case, we're looking to increase the volume (quantity of products) per transaction, or increase the value (the price) of each product or service in the transaction. If you think of this like a shopping cart, we can either get our clients to put more items in the cart or we can increase the price of the items in the cart... or both!

Simple, right? Any time you want to make more money in your business, you now know exactly where to turn: Increase the number of transactions or increase the value per transaction. But it's clearly not that easy to just make this happen, right? If it were, we'd all be rolling in dough!

No, the sticky part of all of this is that we can't directly control what our clients do. We can't simply press a button and increase our transactions or the value of our average sale. The trick here, the great art of all of this, the beating heart of revenue in your business, boils down to your ability to master one simple skill. Can you guess what it is?

You need to influence the behavior of your customers.

This is the key to revenue creation, the key to branding, the key to business growth, and the very definition of marketing. We must master the art of influencing people to buy more, pay more, and tell their friends. That's pretty important, so let me repeat it:

"To create revenue we must master the art of influencing people to buy more, pay more, and refer a friend."

@workingwithdog

Quick Review:

To simplify (you know how much I love a bit of "less is more") here is everything you need to know about revenue creation in a short little list.

1. Our customers or potential customers have needs, wants, and problems.

2. We have a business that that can reduce these pains or increase these pleasures.

3.Because we own businesses (not non-profits), our primary aim is to create revenue. We trade pain-reducing or pleasure-increasing solutions for money: This is a transaction.

4. To generate MORE money (revenue) we can increase the number of transactions or make more per transaction.

5. In order to increase the number of transactions or increase the amount people are willing to pay per transaction (increase revenue), we have to influence the behavior of our clients and potential clients.

6. Everything we do to influence the behavior of our clients or potential clients for the purpose of growing our business (creating revenue or activities that lead to revenue) is marketing.

10. What is Marketing?

Everything that leads to revenue creation in your business, everything that moves you up Million Dollar Dog Brand Mountain, is marketing. Everything. It doesn't even matter if you're aware of it, if you're doing it on purpose, if it's working for or against you – if it in some way, at some point, impacts the revenue in your business, it's marketing.

But what else is it?

Marketing is ads, blogs, social media, copywriting, websites, videos, pricing, customer service, sales, postcards, events, contests, sponsorships... all that stuff we named above that creates revenue. Yup. But what is the definition of marketing? If we're going to embrace it, we should probably give a face to a name right? Well, now you know that marketing involves influencing human behavior in some way... but what IS it?

Google "what is marketing" and Google will tell you marketing is:

"the action or business of promoting and selling products or services, including market research and advertising."[2]
The American Marketing Association defines marketing as:

---

2 https://www.google.es/?gfe_rd=cr&ei=TZepWOa1Nu-J8Qe2uJ_oDA&gws_rd=ssl#q=what+is+marketing]

"the activity, set of institutions, and processes for creating, communicating, delivering, and exchanging offerings that have value for customers, clients, partners, and society at large."[3]
But I think there is something missing from these definitions. Back in America in the '50s when marketing was created, we were a largely unconnected world and marketing was a very linear activity:

1. Company does research to get data
2. Company creates ad based on data
3. Company plans, creates, and releases ad
4. Company measures impact of ad
5. Company makes changes based on measured impact;
6. Company refines and repeats.

To this day, over six decades later, this is STILL the exact same way that many, many companies operate. (And incidentally, this is what they may still teach you if you study marketing at university or in graduate school!) This approach means the company creates and launches, the customer is "targeted," "advertised at," and "sold to." It's a one-way street. From company TO consumer. Research, repeat. In the "good old days," the barriers to entry to get involved in the marketplace were quite high and reaching consumers was quite expensive. This meant that the companies and advertisers held most of the power.

Think of how much our world has changed since the 1950's. This one-way strategy is pre-internet and pre-social media. The timeline for this kind of product and communications planning is not quick either. A new product launch or campaign like this could take MONTHS, sometimes YEARS from start to finish.
From the first strategy meetings, test groups, and market analysis, through the naming and branding process, to ad testing, and on and on.

3 https://www.ama.org/AboutAMA/Pages/Definition-of-Marketing.aspx

Does anyone see a problem with this?

Well first of all, we are obviously getting less and less enchanted with being advertised AT (with the exception the Super Bowl ads where advertising is a cultural event and a form of entertainment). We don't want cookies and pop-ups so we are installing ad-blockers. We don't want annoying commercials every three minutes in our TV shows so we watch Netflix. The reign of disruptive advertising is coming to an end.

This isn't the only change, however; we also want more and more of a say in the choices that go into what we buy: how and where it's made, where the materials come from, what price it's offered at, if we can customize it to our own needs, and certainly, how and where it is sold to us.

In our modern, digitally connected world, the person being marketed to has a say in things: a voice that cannot be ignored. Just ask the black cabs of London about Uber, ask hotels about Airbnb, and ask the major networks about Netflix; if an institution doesn't suit us, we'll circumnavigate it. If we don't like the options presented to us, we'll make our own. Marketing is now a two-way street, and thanks to the internet and social media, barriers to market entry are virtually non-existent and therefore, the power has shifted to the consumer.

Marketing is now a conversation.

"Our people are very passionate; a lot of them are very knowledgeable, and sometimes that are controversial, because I think we need to have these conversations, especially when it comes to using bad techniques and things that cause pain or fear on dogs, which I'm dead-set against. I'll post something like this and you'll get the odd person saying "Victoria Stilwell, you're a jerk!" and that's fine. But our brand only exists to push these conversations forward." –Victoria Stilwell

Let's have a look at some conversations that are relevant to your business, shall we?

"Pit bulls are dangerous" – That's marketing.
"Pit bulls make great family pets" – That's marketing.

These statements represent two opposing sides with different fears and agendas, trying to "brand" the pit bull in two drastically different ways.

How about this one:

"Shelter dogs are unhealthy and damaged."
"Shelter dogs are great, often pure-bred dogs."

Again, all marketing: long-held, culturally integrated belief vs. a new campaign marketing the shelter dog as a healthy, loveable, and worthwhile companion.

These are big topics in the dog world. These may be conversations you care deeply about. They are conversations your customers might be having right this very second! How about these:

"You need to be the pack leader."
"You need to shave your dog in the summer."
"You need to get a pinch collar on that dog to control it."
"You need to get your dog vaccinated."
"You need to feed your dog RAW."

-or-

"Who knows a good local dog walker?"
"Where do you take your dog to be groomed?"
"What products do recommend to keep my dog from pulling?"
"My dog has just been diagnosed with cancer; what do I do?"
"I am getting a puppy next month – where are good puppy classes?"
"Who knows a good resource for learning about RAW?"

Can you see how important it is that you get involved in these conversations? **Your clients need you and the knowledge you can turn into results for them!**

Your customers are out there looking for someone with YOUR exact expertise to help guide them. They are not looking to be sold to, they are looking to be served. To be helped. To get educated.

Now don't be mistaken: Unless they're the quintessential "crazy dog lady" or a big-time dog advocate who is happy to crack open a bottle of wine and debate breed legislation or puppy mills all night, chances are, your clients don't really care about these conversations. They are not engaging in them for fun (it's your colleagues and competitors who do that). No, for your customer, the conversation is just a means to an end. Your customer wants to improve their dog's life and the increase the quality of the time they spend together (or apart).

**Your customer cares about the outcome of the conversation.
They care about results.**

Your potential clients want solutions. They will seek out the stuff that solves their problems or feeds their desires. You are the stuff that solves their problems and feeds their desires. You = results. They are out there looking for you RIGHT NOW!

This is how the conversation (marketing) leads to money in your pocket (revenue). You listen to the needs and desires of your potential clients and you present opportunities to solve them. Sometimes these solutions are free (the valuable content you put out into the world via YouTube, Instagram, your blog, etc.) and sometimes (more likely after consuming your free content, so the client now knows, likes, and trusts you) the client pays you for your products and services. Boom. Transaction!

Notice I haven't yet said a single thing about selling...
Marketing should not be about selling.

Remember, marketing is about influencing human behavior. The "hard sell" is rarely the most influential tool.

You don't need to SELL yourself. You need to SHOW UP as the solution to your customers' problems.

So this is all well and good, but the question then still begs, how do we do it? How do we participate in conversations, how do we create them, how do we influence behavior, how do we do marketing?

I am so glad you asked...

11. The Six Stages of Marketing

It's probably not a great idea to invest in building a brand without understanding exactly how and where it fits in to the marketing of your business in general. To make it easy, I have basically crammed all the basics of "how to do marketing" into six stages. These stages and the formula I am about to teach you is the culmination of over a decade of hands-on experience, post-graduate study, and first-hand research in the pet industry in the US and the UK.

My real-life experience began in 2005 and has ticked on for 12+ years, including co-building Dog is Good and consulting with everyone from one-woman-dog-brands to dog media empires to multi-billion-dollar corporations like PetCo and Purina. That real-life MBA was galvanized during my actual Marketing Master's program in London where I completed a dissertation on Social Media in the Pet Industry and graduated with distinction. Lastly, I compared these real-life and academic theories against the ideas, results and best practices shared by the 10 Million Dollar Dog Brands I interviewed for this book.

Only the most proven, realistic, and relevant-in-our-digital-world stuff made the cut. Please also keep in mind, that I am for entrepreneurs. The marketing stuff I teach in this book is aimed fairly exclusively at small businesses. That doesn't mean it's not helpful for enterprise; it just means that some of the more personally relevant content is not appropriate for larger corporations.

Marketing Stages

I believe there are essentially six stages to marketing. It's probably no great surprise given the title of this book, but the first stage of marketing, the foundation, is largely about branding. After branding, there are five more stages, which are really more about the tactical "doing" part of making the entire MDDB Advantage Cycle come to life. These other stages are the ones you probably think about when you hear the word "marketing." The activities in marketing stages two–six ensure people are actually seeing, using, and engaging with your brand, product, or service. All six stages are important for a brand to achieve optimal results, so although we will be discussing just the first stage in this book, I want to introduce you to all six:

The Six Stages of Marketing

1. **Attract:** Build a brand and platform

2. **Broadcast:** Build awareness

3. **Engage:** Build relationships

4. **Convert:** Get transactions, get repeat purchase and referrals

5. **Measure:** Collect data and analyze

6. **Improve:** Apply data and start again!

Building this framework into the very core of your competencies is your best chance at having a sustainable business with a long list of people lining up to work with you. It's not easy at first, but it's not as hard as you think either. One at a time, you will simply embed processes into your daily business life that involve finding new sales leads, moving them through the stages of the sales funnel, changing them from "stranger" to "friend," and along the way, converting them into happy, chatty, paying clients.

Sales Funnel: From Stranger to Friend

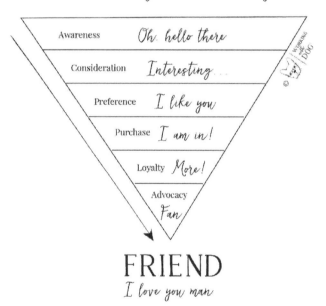

STRANGER

I don't know you. I don't trust you.

Awareness	*Oh, hello there*
Consideration	*Interesting...*
Preference	*I like you*
Purchase	*I am in!*
Loyalty	*More!*
Advocacy	*Fan*

FRIEND

I love you man

The Six Marketing Stages are simply a step-by-step guide for moving potential customers through the sales funnel.

They start out as strangers and we try to get as many of them as possible to turn into buyers, repeat buyers, and word-of-mouth machines. This is pretty basic stuff, but is easily overlooked by many petpreneurs just starting out, especially if nobody ever taught you about sales funnels! If you've never looked at a sales funnel in your business this will be your new favorite diagram. It's an excellent way to understand how and why people actually hire you or buy from you. **It's a process.**

It usually doesn't happen in one moment or action – it's a journey from never having heard of you, to eventually buying from you. Even if they happen upon your business at an event, have never heard of you before, and do end up purchasing from you in that moment, it's important to understand that inside that head of theirs, they are moving through the stages of the sales funnel in quick succession.

This is a powerful insight to have because now that you understand their mental and emotional journey, you know how to craft your booth, your website, your blog, your advertisements – how to craft the tools you need to help them move from "I don't know you, I don't trust you" to "I love you, man!"

Stage 1: Attract

- Find out why you do what you do, who you do it for, and craft why-based messaging that your who cannot ignore -

I am an extremely visual person and I love me some strategy, so the first stage of marketing is my favorite. But even if you're not a visual person and you're not into strategy, don't worry. In the next chapter, and throughout the rest of this book, I am going to break down the mysterious magic of the "attract" stage of marketing into a simple formula you can follow. The Million Dollar Dog Brand Formula. Once you're done with that, the next step will be go to find people to woo!

Stage 2: Discover

- Find more of your who to fill the funnel -

Now that you know why you do what you do and who you do it for and have crafted a brand and messaging that your ideal clients will love, it's time to go find those potential clients. This is largely a research and trial-and-error phase, where you find out where your people are and what channels are effective for reaching them. This is one of the most mysterious stages, where you are in a nearly constant state of experimentation, measurement, and iteration.

Stage 3: Engage

- Make your who fall in love with you -

This is one of the most important (and often ignored) stages in marketing. Engaging is all about starting conversations: creating and sharing content with your target audience. This is not a hard sell, it won't always be about YOU at all.

We want to generously offer valuable content and insights on topics that will interest our potential customers. This stage is all about building relationships. Wooing your who.

Stage 4: Convert

- Pop the question -

"Once a year we have a dollar pet ID sale. We started this five years ago. The third year, we weren't planning on doing it at all and then two days before National Dog Day we started getting emails, about a dozen of them, saying, "Is your sale in two days? I've been waiting for this!" Then it was a scramble to get everything ready. Basically it's a coupon that is a huge discount on all the IDs. It wasn't just the sales; the real benefit was in getting our name out and getting people talking about it. The people who talk the most about it were the people who are likely the best word of mouth for us. It's the shelters, it's the rescues, it's the people who are passionate about what we're doing. So, find the people who are passionate about what you're doing and find how to get to them. Because what they do is they share the heck out of it on social media, and I mean last year I think we sold 3000 or something like that in one day."

-Lorien, PetHub

A conversion is the process of causing something to change – you want your audience to ACT! Our favorite tools to increase conversions are: Powerful Promotions (no, a 10% discount is NOT enough), Urgency and Scarcity (add a bit of positive pressure) and word of mouth (get your happy customers helping new customers say yes for the first time).

Stage 5: Measure

- Keep track of what works-

"We said, 'Huh, let's start really looking at the data folks and looking at where our customers are coming from with the highest ROI, lowest cost per acquisition, and let's truly dig into the data and see where it is.' We realized that the channel that everyone else said, "Oh you need to go for this channel, you need to go for this channel," was not the right channel for us and that the channel that everyone said, "Oh there is no money there," was actually the channel that had the most promise of us." - Lorien, PetHub

The only way to know what's working is to be able to measure it. Of course one could argue you can never measure ENOUGH but there is a point where it becomes overwhelming for most entrepreneurs. If you're not regularly looking at your web or sales data, you are definitely leaving money on the table (and possibly costing yourself extra time and resources) so embedding this in your business habits becomes one of the most critical pieces to achieving those lovely brand advantages. Equally, if you're hiring people, teams, or businesses to help with your marketing efforts - hire someone who insists that everything they do for you be measurable!

Stage 6: Improve

-The difference between where you are now
and where you want to be. Winning isn't free -

This is often the most neglected stage because we're all "too busy"! First, fix the problems – get the basics working consistently.

Then, optimize the basics – reduce friction. Next, scale your successes. When you find something that works, scale it up! Finally, once you know the basics are covered and working well, look for new opportunities.

Does all of this sound a bit overwhelming?

Relax. Understanding and getting good at all this stuff won't happen overnight. Remember, these stages are a long-term guide, not a to-do list for this week! In reality, these stages happen all at the same time, not in tidy succession, so if you already have a business, you're probably already dealing with elements of each of these stages almost every day.

If you want exact how-to's, do's and don'ts, and 24/7 access to a support system that "gets it," then get into Working with Dog. We talk about this stuff with each other and our expert contributors every day. We answer your questions live. We attend conferences and regularly talk shop with industry-leading know-it-alls, so we've got all the marketing genius you need, on tap. Certainly, we are much stronger together than apart, so consider joining us at workingwithdog.com/join.

"First the why,

then the who,

then plan,

then do."

@workingwithdog

12. The Six Marketing Senses

I want you to stop for a minute. Clear your brain of all its busy thoughts, all the stuff you've just read and all the ideas spinning around and picture a young, healthy, happy dog. I want you to imagine that dog running at full speed through a field of tall, lush grass and leaping into the air to catch, at the perfect moment, at the perfect angle, a bright orange frisbee. The dog makes the catch and lands on its feet, tossing its head back and forth slightly, prancing around and wagging its tail, thrilled with his successful catch.

Now rewind for a second and think about that dog up close, in slow motion. Think about all the synapses firing in his brain, the muscle sinews tightening, his lungs and heart pumping hard to refresh his body with oxygen, the narrowing of his pupils as his eyes focus on the toy, the sensors in the nose going crazy detecting scents in the air, the twisting of his spine, the reaching of his paws, the opening of his mouth as all of the molecules of this dog reach the exact right point at the exact right millisecond to grab the frisbee from the air.

Pretty impressive stuff, right? In order for this dog to make this catch, all of his senses need to be optimized, firing together to help him reach his target. This dog is the perfect metaphor for your brand. It's not enough to be alive as a business; you need to be fully optimized as a brand.

For your performance to peak, to catch that frisbee, **your senses need to be honed.**

The Method and The Magic

Your roadmap to building your Million Dollar Dog Brand is broken down into six essential steps, that we call the Six Marketing Senses. Embedded in these steps are traditional marketing musts like targeting, positioning, market analysis, developing a USP and a value proposition, a product and pricing strategy, etc. Let's call this stuff the method. But also embedded in these steps is the stuff that can't be measured: the passion, the aspirational appeal, the X-Factor that separates the good from the great. Let's call this stuff the magic. Earlier, I said that brand building is more like alchemy than science and that is because it is equal parts method and magic. Don't be foolish enough to think that you can do it with just one half. You can't. You need both the data-driven science and the juicy intangible energetic stuff to build a Million Dollar Dog Brand. This means it is likely you will need support to offset your left-brained or right-brained self along the way. Prepare yourself now for the idea of hiring people to help you with the bits where you're not especially skilled.

The Process

The Six Marketing Senses is a sequentially ordered process, a secret formula to creating a Million Dollar Dog Brand: a sensational product and a sensational brand simultaneously. The steps might be simple, but they are not easy.

This is not a "fill in the blanks over the weekend" kind of process. For this journey to be fruitful, you're going to have to give it time. You're going to have to have patience. You're going to suffer and struggle. But if you stick with it, you will also experience joy, sublime relief and probably an almost manic state of amazing idea generation. If you stick with the steps, you will have an exact blueprint of your Million Dollar Dog Brand, with all the perks and freedoms it promises.

Six Marketing Senses

1. **Sense of Self** (why)
2. **Sense of Sight** (who)
3. **Sense of Hearing** (what)
4. **Sense of Touch** (where)
5. **Sense of Smell** (how part 1)
6. **Sense of Taste** (how part 2)

First the why, then the who, then plan, then do.

Please keep in mind that what we're talking about here is strategy. It's the plan creation. The icing. It's what comes before doing, it is not the doing itself. You will be responsible for acting on this plan to make this magic come to life. You'll have to bake the cake. That's all you. The bad news is, you can't force it or rush it, which will frustrate you at times. The good news is, if you do these steps correctly, with the time and consideration they deserve, they will propel you so hard through the doing that you almost won't have a choice. Your "I can't" will become "I have to," and your "This is too hard" will become "How can I do more, faster?" It's a thrilling transformation that I can't wait for you to experience. Many of my clients have described it as a "click." Suddenly, everything just clicks into place. It's clear, it's deliciously appealing, and you feel ready to step into your role as the leader of this Million Dollar Dog Brand. Your assignment is to not settle.

Don't settle with "good enough"; keep pushing until you feel the click. Keep pushing until you know, not think, but feel, deep in your bones, you've found your Million Dollar Dog Brand.

Want some help?

I built workingwithdog.com so brand builders like you would have somewhere to turn to get help on the way up the mountain.

Join us and you will get access to our amazingly empowering community of petpreneurs, many of who have already conquered, or are currently going through these six steps. This group has proven to be an incredible support system for people just like you and there really is nothing else like it for brave, like-minded souls building a pet brand instead of just a pet business.

Come on over to workingwithdog.com/join/.

"People don't buy WHAT you do. They buy WHY you do it."

– Simon Sinek

13. Sense One: Sense of Self

"89% of American and 84% of British consumers say they are loyal to brands that share their values."[4]

What Is It?

The first of our Marketing Senses, the Sense of Self, is where any sensational product or a sensational brand created by an entrepreneur finds its emotional core.

This is the conscious or unconscious obsession or fixation that drives you; it's the lifestyle that created the problem you feel compelled to solve. It's the group of people, social movement, place, hobby, or tribe you proudly stand up for. Well call this sense your "why." We are going to spend the most time and pages on this first sense because it is infinitely the most important, and also potentially the most difficult to wrap your head around. Finding, claiming, and expertly communicating your "why" is your very first opportunity to show up as a brand instead of a business and it all starts with one very simple question:

---

4 http://blog.accessdevelopment.com/index.php/2013/11/the-ultimate-collection-of-loyalty-statistics

Why do you do what you do?

Although it appears quite straightforward, do not be fooled! It is not easy to answer this question like a Purple Dog. It is actually quite difficult to answer this question in a way that makes you sensational.

"When I was growing up, we had dogs we ran around the neighborhood with, but we didn't often take them places. In my '20s, my dogs accompanied me on adventures: backpacking, skiing, mountain biking, and kayaking. The dogs were great companions but they were travelling around with us, far from home, in these harsh environments: scree, hot sand, or in riparian environments with lots of water and rocks. We were asking them to perform at a higher level but without any protection. Meanwhile we've got our lifejacket, our hiking boots, this amazing bike helmet on, and they're running around just as they would at home. What has helped me over the years is to relate to individuals with the idea that when we're taking dogs into a new environment, they benefit from some protection. The opportunity to create gear for dogs really comes from the value people get from using the gear. It's nice to make something that people want and that people enjoy using. That is what has really fueled my drive: I love creating solutions that address specific needs. It's a really rewarding experience. My soul is fed from my outdoor activities and dogs seem to thrive in these outdoor activities too, so it seems to be a great relationship. It continues to feed everybody, I think." – Patrick, Ruffwear

"There was really no plan, it was just a craft, it was just a hobby and it was a form of occupational therapy. My doctor said, "It's going to take a really long time for you to get well. You're going to survive, you're going to live, so just do something gentle that you love." And I thought, "Well I love dogs and I love working with my hands, and I love making stuff. Why don't I just keep making more stuff?" That's how Harry Barker started: It was a hand-crafted love of being a maker and a giver and a lover of pets and people. I'm a crafty little maker at heart and I didn't really set out to have a million-dollar business. I didn't know it was a million-dollar idea."
– Carol, Harry Barker

"I was with a charity called Cause for Paws where we would really get rescue dogs from the municipal shelters before they were put down and get them new homes. My husband and I started to foster as well (around 40 dogs and cats in two years). I was just so sick of the waste of life I was seeing. Literally thousands, and thousands, and thousands of animals being put down in the municipal shelters every year in Manhattan and the five Burroughs. I wanted to get my training information out to a large audience. By this time we'd moved out to New Jersey and I'd become a mom. But I still wasn't satisfied in the small reach that I had. Then, when my daughter was eight months old and I was putting her to bed one night, I sat down exhausted and turned the television, and the first episode of the Supernanny was airing. And I remember looking at that and going, "Oh my goodness, this is what I do but with dogs. The same approach that Jo Frost, the Supernanny had with kids: firm, but fair and kind, I had the same with dogs. So I emailed the producers of the Supernanny my idea, and the next day they called me. Three months later, I was filming the pilot for It's Me or the Dog." – Victoria Stilwell, Positively.com

Why Does It Matter?

The fundamental difference between a business and a brand comes down to how they choose to show up; how they communicate. A business shows up as a business trying to sell, a brand shows up as humans trying to help. In the world we're in now, where we don't want to be sold to, which one do you think has a better chance of being successful long-term?

How do you differentiate between the two?

A business tries to connect with your logic.
A brand tries to connect with your emotions.

When most of us set out to sell something, we start with the most obvious and work our way in. We tell you what the thing is, how it's made, how it works, and why you might need it. We tell you all the facts and figures about what makes it a superior thing and then we tell you a price. Simple. You should have all the information you need to make your decision, right?

Well yes, it is simple... and obvious... and marginally effective. If people need the thing they will seek out the information, compare your thing against other things and probably choose the middle-priced one, the cheapest one or the best of the best depending on what they value (some people just buy the most expensive thing because it "must be the best" and they don't want to take time to do the research, whereas some people buy the thing that looks the best, etc.). But this strategy leaves you very vulnerable to the company that comes out with the same thing but better, for a better price. So how do you compete?

Don't sell "what," sell "why."

We start at the less obvious: We describe the scenario we think you're hoping for if you buy the thing – we paint a picture of WHY you need it – we stimulate your senses using imagery, color, video and music and we suck you in to a moment, a feeling, then we present our thing as the essential missing link between your present and this ideal future. As a side-note, we also offer all the practical info you're looking for about the "how" and the "what" and then we present the price.

When we start with "why" rather than "what" we tap into the emotional decision-making part of the brain. When we sell a vision or a belief rather than facts and figures, we give our customers a powerful reason to say yes.
Suddenly, they don't need to check the competition – they're even willing to pay more because they KNOW this is the thing for them. This strategy is a magnet for the people who are attracted to the vision you are selling – the people who believe what you believe. This strategy is very, very difficult to compete with, which is what makes your "why" the core of your "sustainable competitive advantage."

A business tries to persuade you using facts, figures and logic.
A brand tries to connect emotionally with you based on a shared belief.

A business sells.
A brand helps.

A business is obsessively focused on ROI (return on investment).
A brand is obsessively focused on the customer's experience.

A business makes decisions based on data, shareholders' opinions, and projections.

A brand makes decisions based on data, customer feedback, and gut feelings.

A business builds in control and approval over every word and every decision.
A brand builds a values-based team and a culture that can think for itself.

A business builds policies.
A brand builds relationships.

A business operates defensively.
A brand operates abundantly.

A business has fear.
A brand has faith.

A business's competitive advantage is based on features and price.
A brand's competitive advantage is based on trust.

A business starts with WHAT.
A brand starts with WHY.

You might have heard you need to sell "the benefits" of your product or service, not the "features." One lecturer in my Master's program described this concept well with this example:

"If your company sells drills, understand that your customers don't really care about the make, model, power, or design of the drill – all they care about is the hole in the wall. Don't sell the drill, sell the hole." – Adam Raman

The Science behind the Why

In a 2009 Ted Talk,[5] Simon Sinek introduced the concept of "the golden circle," which explains why this "connecting emotionally" with our clients leading to purchase concept, works. In his research, Sinek uncovered that the most profoundly successful influencers and industry leaders all had this same strategy in common:

They didn't sell what they did, they sold why they did it. They connected emotionally instead of logically with their audience.

The Golden Circle

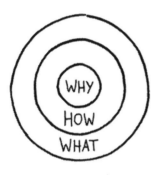

What
Every organization on the planet knows WHAT they do. These are products they sell or the services they offer.

How
Some organizations know HOW they do it. These are the things that make them special or set them apart from their competition.

Why
Very few organizations know WHY they do what they do. WHY is not about making money. That's a result. It's a purpose, cause or belief. It's the very reason your organization exists.

© 2013 Simon Sinek, Inc.

CREDIT: SIMON SINEK, INC. WWW.STARTWITHWHY.COM

But the really interesting part is that the science behind this powerful truth is found in our biology: It's mapped-out in our brain. If you take a cross-section of the our brain and look at it from the top down, you'll find these layers like concentric circles.

At the core, you'll find the limbic brain – containing the "why" and "how" – this is the part responsible for decision making, but not capable of language. This is why when you're trying to decide but you think, "This doesn't feel right," there is something in this limbic brain shouting, "No, no, no!" even if you're rational brain, the outer neocortex, can logically connect the dots and say, "Yes, yes, yes." We make decisions with the emotional mammal core of our brain, not the rational human bit. For better or worse, it's going to be the way we feel, not what we think, that is going to influence our decision-making behavior.

So how are you going to show up?
Show up as the solution that feels right.

This is not just a theory.

This whole "lead with why" concept has been validated over and over with consumer research, including this study published in the Harvard Business Review:

"A shared value is a belief that both the brand and consumer have about a brand's higher purpose or broad philosophy. Of the consumers in our study who said they have a brand relationship, 64% cited shared values as the primary reason. Many brands have a demonstrable higher purpose baked into their missions, whether it's Patagonia's commitment to the environment or Harley Davidson's goal "to fulfill dreams through the experience of motorcycling." These feel authentic to consumers, and so provide a credible basis for shared values and relationship-building. To build relationships, start by clearly communicating your brand's philosophy or higher purpose."[6]

---

6 https://hbr.org/2012/05/three-myths-about-customer-eng

Hint: Your brand's philosophy or higher purpose is the "why." We'll talk about the relationship bit later...

The Lesson:
If you take away nothing from this book except the following truth, I will consider my job well done: If we want to be able to charge more (make more profit) and maintain a sustainable competitive advantage (last longer) we need to show up as a brand, not a business.

We need to start with the WHY not the WHAT.
We need to be fundamentally human and help, focusing on relationships rather than being robotic and selling, focusing solely on transactions.

What Are You Going to Stand For?

The facts of biology and proof in history lead us to conclude that to be profitable and sustainable, we need to show up as the choice that feels right to our ideal clients. Sure, that's all well in good, but how on earth do we know what feels right to a bunch of strangers? We can't read their mind – we can't possibly be everything to everyone – where do we begin?

Well I am not going to lie to you, this is the hard part. This is the moment when most entrepreneurs shut down, switch off, pick a generic business name, grab a logo with a paw print on it, make a decently effective product, copy the strategy or pricing or tactics of someone who's been doing it while for longer, and call it a day.

This may work to start a functional business, but this does NOT a brand build! If all you want is to spend your precious time doing something more palatable than commuting to a cubicle, this may just cut it. You may even stumble onto a winning formula where you can pay the mortgage and not want to cry yourself to sleep when new competitors pop up. It's totally possible, but given my experience, not very likely.

What is MORE likely is that you'll invest a lot of time, a lot of money, a lot of ego and a lot of love into something that either fizzles out when it gets too hard / expensive / crowded in the marketplace or you will fantastically burn out in a blaze of glory when you make yourself sick, ruin a relationship, or simply hit a brick wall you can't climb over.

How do I know this? Because businesses who don't know who they are or who they're for struggle to find clients, struggle to get paid, and struggle to get seen / heard / discovered.
As we all know, making less revenue does not mean your costs go away, or that you suddenly have less obligations to tend to – it just means your stress, panic and desperate decision-making increases as you sink closer and closer to your point of no return: your breaking point. Plus, desperation stinks and your clients can smell it on you. So the more you gasp for air, the less and less likely you are to turn it all around.

I think we can all agree this is a fate we'd like to avoid, yes? Maybe you've already experienced this downward spiral and that's why you're here? I don't want to bum you out; I want to keep my promise to be real with you. The reality is that if you build a business instead of a brand, you're likely to vanish into obscurity. Not definitely, but your path will be so much harder for you than it will be for the brand next door, and you may come out the other side, back at that cubicle.

Put Your Why in Action

Everything worth having is hard. Hard does not mean impossible, and it doesn't even mean miserable – it just means it's going to take effort. As an entrepreneur, the first step in building a brand is to understand yourself: what you want and what you believe in. You can't sell someone else on this vision if you don't know what it is. Be brave enough to invest yourself fully in this process and you will be rewarded a thousand times over!!

How Does Your "Why" Show Up?

Now, I know what you're thinking. You think you've found your why and it was super easy: You love dogs. You want to make life better for them. You want to "enhance the relationship between dogs and their people" – hooray! You've done it – profound soul-searching exercise complete. Drop the mic and exit stage left, right?

Wrong.

Almost every dog business has this "why." If you want to build a Million Dollar Dog Brand it is not enough to tick the box with something this obvious. You have got to dig deeper. You've got to find the place where your dog-related passion meets other elements, resources, skills, experience, and desires that are unique **to YOU** or your business.

Selling Around the Edge of Your Business

Last year I met a wonderful gal at a conference I attended in London. Her name is Janet Murray (@jan_murray). She is a journalist and PR expert who works with small businesses. She described this concept a really lovely way. Although she wasn't talking about branding, she was talking about how to get published or featured in press, the concept is the same. She suggests "telling stories around the edge of your business." I'll explain.

In case you didn't already know this, journalists are not interested in what you sell. They don't care at all. They are interested in stories. In web traffic. In kudos from their editor.

On the flip side, the only reason you want PR is to sell more. **Am I right?**

So the secret (like pretty much any relationship, I suppose) is to give to get. In this case, to tell stories (pitch interesting story ideas) that are related to the edges of your business; the places where what you sell intersects with your life, beliefs, hobbies, personal stories, experiences and relationships in interesting ways. This is your "hook"; this is what you pitch.[7]

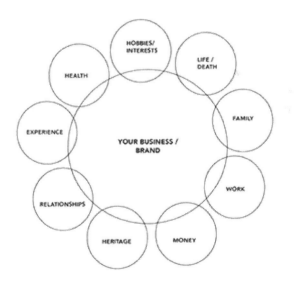

7 https://pbs.twimg.com/media/CIUXarCWEAEjzHA.jpg]

Why? Because journalists do not care about the features of your latest product and neither do their readers, but they might just care about you overcoming a horrible illness to build your business, or making something out of nothing while single parenting, or the innovations in technology you're using to run your business. You give a good story, they give you editorial coverage that is actually interesting and that actually sucks people in to your "why."

Purple dogs do this all the time. They don't settle for the same rhetoric every other pet business uses, like "for Pet Owners who love their pet'" (how generic is that, that is literally EVERY Pet Owner in the world – what a terrible non-niche!) Aw hell no!

Purple dogs find stories at the edge of that obvious why and add to it. They put their own spin on it. Their "why" is at the intersection of "pet and human relationship" and their individual products, competencies, and beliefs. I encourage you to visit the websites of these Million Dollar Dog Brands and use their examples as inspiration to dig out your own unique, specific threads about why you do what you do. Yes, you're for dogs and their people, but what else?

What Kind of Brand Do You Want?

Before you start to dig too deeply into your why, you need to decide what kind of brand you want to be. In this context, when I say what kind I mean do you want to be building a **personal brand** (you and your personality are the brand) or a **general brand** (a brand built around a product, service, or lifestyle).

Just to clear up any confusion, both of these brand types can be considered **lifestyle brands** because a lifestyle brand (a term that I notice is getting thrown around a lot these days) is simply a brand that promotes a particular lifestyle.

It can be a person who promotes that lifestyle, or a product / service that does. The alternative to a lifestyle brand is what I call a **concept brand**, which is built purely on a technology, function, product, or service. Usually concept brands are reverse-engineered around a product. I expect most of you will be building personal lifestyle or general lifestyle brands.

There are pros and cons to both personal and general brands, the most obvious being that one of them is tied to you directly. You can choose to build a bit of a mix, but you want to be clear which is the priority so you don't get muddled or confused.

If you're a solopreneur and you can't decide which brand you're building, you can even try starting with a general brand and putting your name alongside it (a bit like I have done with Working with Dog). You can simply add a YOUR BRAND NAME with YOUR NAME HERE or YOUR BRAND NAME by YOUR NAME HERE or just put them together like Victoria Stilwell Positively.

How to Master the "Why" Sense

It doesn't matter whether you're creating a personal brand or a general brand; as an entrepreneur your most compelling "why" in business will be **anchored in what drives you as a person**. This is partly because we pour so much of ourselves into our brands, that if they're aligned with what we believe, it feels a lot less like work. The whole marketing piece becomes much easier if you're talking and writing and shouting about stuff you really are interested in and care about, rather than stuff you're supposed to write and care about. **Make sense?**

So, now we are going to find and shift the lid off the deep well of compelling dreams, desires, passions, and emotions that you will continually draw from in order to grow and sustain your sensational brand. No pressure :)

Below I have included the exercise I have all my clients go through called the Why Map. This is the very first place to start when trying to uncover the emotional core that will drive your brand.

Go easy on yourself as you explore – it's not a process that can be rushed and you will probably go through several iterations of "what your brand stands for" as you get more clear and concise. You may find yourself doing the Why Map exercise several times before you move on, or doing it once and moving straight on, and then revisiting it much later and starting over again. You know you've got it when you don't just like the sound of what you've come up with... you feel it. You feel it in your guts and in your bones. You'll get there, stick with it!

Why Mapping

Discovering the deep, rich inner workings of what motivates you as a person and as a business owner starts with the very simple step of acknowledging what you have. Who are you? What are your skills? What are your values? What are your resources? Even the things that may seem like disadvantages can actually be sources of competitive advantage – anything that makes you you might be part of what makes you hard to compete with!

Before you picked up this book, I expect that most of you had an idea of what you do. Either you already do it, sell it, or you have a strong idea of what the service or product is that you want to do or sell. Yes? For now, I want you to set that aside. I don't want you to think about your grooming business or your gorgeous doggy sweaters. As much as humanly possible,

I want you to set aside who you think you are based on what you do. This is hard because we put so much weight on what we do to define who we are.

They are NOT the same thing. I want you to do this exercise as a human being, not a human doing! Who are YOU... deep down... at your core, not just at the moment. Pretend you don't have a job or a business and start from scratch. Don't try to force yourself into an existing box; give yourself permission to do this exercise without any pre-conceived notions. Ok? Ok!

"I barely graduated high school and I was dyslexic and had ADD. I didn't go to art school. If you look at my resume on paper, I have no talent, I have no marketable skills. Other than a panty model and a fire-eater. Now I'm too old to model and I've done fire-eating, thank you. I don't know how it is I do what I do, but it's authentic and it's real and it comes from inside and I think everyone has that potential." – Carol, Harry Barker

1. Acknowledging your Resources

I'd like you to use a notebook, your computer, your phone – whatever feels easiest – to write a long, meandering list of the following:

Skills: What can you DO?
Assets: What do you OWN?
Expertise: What do you KNOW?
Reputation: What do people KNOW about YOU?
Relationships: WHO do you know?
Influence: What can you get OTHER PEOPLE to do?
Values: What do you BELIEVE in?
Hobbies: How do you ENJOY spending your TIME?

Some questions to consider to help you brainstorm:

What advantages do I have over others?
What disadvantages do I have that other people might relate to?

What sets me apart from my competitors?

Why would a customer be drawn to ME and what I do?

What have my work, education, experience or struggles taught me that I can use in my business?

What do I like best about myself?

What do I like best about what I make / sell / do?

What am I best at in life, not just business?

What is it that people always ask me to help them out with?

What is my favorite way to spend my time?

What feels easy for me?

Who do I enjoy working with?

Try to set money-making out of your mind and consider:

If I won the lottery, what would I do?

Go crazy with this. When you come up with something, keeping asking yourself, "Yes, but why?" You might find yourself winding all the way back to childhood traumas or deeply held beliefs or needs you have... that's great! That's exactly the kind of work I'd love you to do here: Find out what REALLY makes you tick and what REALLY is motivating your decision making! Gaining this level of awareness is the first step in being able to harness all of that raw emotional stuff for the benefit of your brand!

2. Mapping the Why

The next step in the dig for your why is to take that long list of "why" ideas you've just brainstormed and list them out, one word or short phrase at a time, in three columns. You can do this old-school style with a pen and paper, or in a digital document, but either way you're going to need to cut it up so make sure you can (maybe don't do this bit in your favorite journal). So you're going to take the ideas from your existing list, and if you can, add even more, asking yourself these questions:

Why do the work I do?

What moves me?

What or who do I feel compelled to defend / protect?

What gifts do I have?

What gives me a natural high?

Why do I get up in the morning?

What am I really proud of?

If I could spend 100 hours in a library learning about a topic, what would it be?

Where is my happy place?

What do I love talking to other people about?

How do I express myself?

What recharges my batteries?

What does freedom look like, taste like, smell like?

What makes me feel in "the flow"?

What am I passionate about changing in the world?

Imagine this like a grid. Fill it out one word at a time and keep each one short (one or two words) and very specific.

NEXT: Cut the sheets into the individual cells with each word on its own. Cut them all until you have little tiny why bits that you can play with.

THEN: You're going to sort these little scraps of paper in whatever way is clear to you. By topic... by type... what seems to go together? Start to make piles or columns of the ideally matched things. (This exercise really is easier by physically moving bits of paper around rather than trying to do it digitally, so definitely give it a go the analog way!)

LAST: Move your words around and combine or clarify your piles until you have between four to eight of them. Give each one a name based on what is in the pile. Either type or tape them into columns with headers of their category name. What categories do you have? Which one is the most full? Did you struggle to find any pattern? Did you come up with anything that surprised you? What did you learn? Willing to share? We'd love to see your why map: www.facebook.com/workingwithdog.

Practical "Why" Tools

Once you complete the why mapping exercise, or at least get it to a stage you're happy to keep playing with, the next steps are to create the following four tools. These tools will help you keep your "why" at the core of everything you do as a brand. Partly, this will make it easier to avoid creating mind-numbing marketing materials that sound just like everyone else's, and partly, it will make the constant decision-making and filtering you have to do much easier. These tools make it super clear what is and is not a good fit for your brand.

These four brand strategy elements will serve you again and again so do prioritize completing them, especially if you'd like your investments in things like ads, a new logo, your website, PR campaigns, event booths etc. to result in the best possible returns.

The Four "Why" Tools Are:

1. **Brand Pillars**
2. **Brand Statement**
3. **Brand Voice**
4. **Brand Story**

1. Brand Pillars

"We're not very different than we were when we started in 1997. We still have our same five core values and those are: Philanthropy, Generosity, Relationships, Fun and Social Responsibility. So we use those five core values in everything that we do."
– Stephanie, Planet Dog

"We formed our pillars, Protect, Share, Nurture, within eight months or so of me coming on board six years ago, but the problem then was we said, "These are our pillars, this is our mission statement," but we didn't really follow it. But then, at the beginning of last year we worked with an advisor who really just told us, "Pull your head out," but in the most wonderful way. Now we are so laser focused and we have our four core goals that at every opportunity that comes our way, if it doesn't beautifully fit into one of our four core goals, we say no. No matter how sexy it is. And we have had some pretty darn sexy things come our way." Lorien, PetHub

The very first tools that will help you keep your why front-and-center in your marketing are your brand pillars. Unfortunately, there is no right way to determine what your brand pillars are, and as Lorien mentions, they're only useful if they're meaningful and they make sense to you. Otherwise, you won't use them!

Remember, we're dealing with alchemy here. The simplest way I can explain it is to say that your brand pillars are your "why" broken down into individual categories that make it actionable. A bit of a mix between "what you're interested in," "why you do what you do," "your brand values," and your "products, services, features or benefits."

HINT: Your brand pillars might be the categories you came up with in your Why Mapping exercise. They might not be, but that's a great place to start looking for inspiration!

The Brand Pillars for Working with Dog are:

- Freedom
- Dogs
- Branding
- Relationships
- Entrepreneurship
- Media

HINT: If your brand is on Pinterest, this is a great way to brainstorm, engage with, and create inspiration around your brand pillars. If you visit our Pinterest page you can see how we've woven our pillars in to our boards: pinterest.com/withdog/.

Some companies create a list of brand values or guiding principles. Brand pillars are a somewhat similar, except as you can see above, they might not all be values or principles. Equally, whereas it's quite natural to share your brand values outright on your website, your brand pillars aren't really something you share with your customers. You don't need to explain them. They will show up in everything you do: your products; your marketing; and your communication with customers, press, staff, and colleagues. You'll find that once you outline what your brand pillars are, they are almost immediately present in any conversation about your business. They're just too integral!

How do I know when they're right?

There is no right and wrong, but you want your brand pillars to be broad enough to stay true no matter what new products or services you might add. So avoid going too specific on the services you offer now, but be specific enough that they are unique to you and your business and not everyone else who does a similar job or sells a similar product.

This is a tough process to navigate alone, so don't forget we are available at Working with Dog to help! One of the best ways to work through this stuff is to sign-up at workingwithdog.com/join and hop in the private Facebook group to start getting feedback from our members.

All of our members are going through this process or have already gone through it - they can relate and they can offer valuable insights! Plus, I'm there too and I'll be happy to help brainstorm with you. This is my area of genius :)

2. Brand Statement

The next step in packing all of that swirling, crazy awesomeness you have bouncing around in your brain into a compelling, commercially viable, authentic, Million Dollar Dog Brand, is to craft a simple statement that describes what your brand stands for. Knowing your brand pillars can help, as some of them may find their way into your brand statement (see my example below). If it's easier, you can start with the simple exercise of creating a mission statement, which goes a little something like this:

[Insert name of brand]'s mission is to [make / build / offer / create] that [what purpose does it serve]

That "what purpose does it serve" bit is where your why really comes into play. That's the bit where you need to understand why you do what you do, so you can insert it succinctly here.

For example, in the early days at Dog is Good before our message was very refined, our Mission was:

"Create and market stylish and clever products that celebrate and enhance the dog-human relationship."

Not all together inspiring or succinct, but it made sense to us at the time and it made it clear what we did and why. We would actually use that exact language when asked what Dog is Good was... but it always felt clunky and awkward to me. Not very human! As we got more clear on why we did what we did, it became:

"Deliver Dogvergnügen (The joy you feel in the presence of Dog)."

We used this statement for years, and I knew it was connecting with people when I received an email someone sent me which included a tattoo of the Dogvergnügen graphic I'd created showing a stick-figure human and dog. But eventually the weird made-up word "Dogvergnugen" became a bit too cumbersome, so the mission has evolved to the simpler brand statement:

"Sharing how great it feels to live life with Dog."

A mission statement, although a bit old school, is a simple and important way to focus what you do (and don't do) and why. But it's kind of boring, right? I mean sure, it's probably going to live on your "about page" somewhere, but when you meet someone for the first time, is that really how you're going to describe what you do? I hope not because you'll sound like a robot. Promise me you won't be that guy!

I suggest boiling that mission statement down even further to a single brand statement that just gets right to the heart of what you do. To maximize impact, aim for a statement that is four to five words, but no more than 10. I don't care what you call this, how it's formatted, if it's straightforward, playful, or sentimental – but you absolutely have to know what you do and to be able to say it in one clear, concise, compelling statement. Often your brand statement is what you answer when someone asks you, "What do you do?" Your brand statement should have a good mix of information and personality.

Why? Because people want to KNOW what you do (information) and you want them to like you instantly (personality) – so take some risks here – use conversational, non-marketingy language. Be purple!

You can see above how Dog is Good's mission statement has evolved into a shorter, more conversational brand statement. In addition, we have always used the tagline "Inspired by Dog" – which is also easy to say, spell, and remember. The personality bit is that it references our play on the use of "Dog" as "God" - which is a theme throughout the brand. So sometimes when asked what the brand is or what we made, I'd simply say, "We make stuff for humans inspired by Dog."

Now that I live in London I don't work at Dog is Good anymore, so these days when someone asks me what I do, this is how I answer them:

I help build pet brands that humans crave.

If I am talking about what I do in relation to workingwithdog.com, which is specifically for entrepreneurs, I say:

I help petpreneurs find freedom by building brands.

All these statements are a mix of information and personality: a bit of what and why. Now, let's have a look at the brand statements of our Million Dollar Dog Brands.

Million Dollar Dog Brand Statements

This is the perfect opportunity to properly introduce you to the Million Dollar Dog Brands featured in this book. It is no coincidence that the ten brands that made the cut all know why they do what they do. Below I have listed each MDDB alongside their brand or mission statements. Notice, as I mentioned previously, that even though all of these companies have a "why" based around "the dog-human relationship," each company has managed to find a unique angle specific to its individual product offering and brand.

1. DOG IS GOOD: www.dogisgood.com

Tagline: "Inspired by Dog"

Brand Statement: Sharing how great it feels to live life with Dog.

2. RUFFWEAR: www.ruffwear.com

Tagline: "Gear for the dogs on the go"

Mission / Brand Statement: Build dog gear to enhance and inspire exploration for outdoor adventurers with their human companions.

3. ZEE DOG: www.zee-dog.com

Tagline / Brand Statement: Connecting Dogs and People.

This mission is especially clever because zee.dog makes leashes and collars – so they quite literally connect dogs to their people! But of course, this mission shows up figuratively as well as the company supports adoption and many initiatives that allow dogs and people to get and stay together.

4. PLANET DOG: www.planetdog.com

Tagline: "Think globally, Act Doggedly"

Brand Statement: Amuse, Explore, Innovate, Create, Philanthropate, and Celebrate - all in the name of the dog.

Planet Dog's promise is a two-way split between social causes and product quality (uncompromising design and functionality with minimal environmental impact). They show up for your dog and your planet simultaneously and they literally guarantee it.

5. VICTORIA STILWELL: www.positively.com
Tagline: "The Future of Dog Training"
Mission / Brand Statement: Changing Dogs' Lives Positively.

Everything Victoria creates, says, does, collaborates on, and cares about promotes this mission – she eats, sleeps, and breathes it. This brand is all about dog welfare and social change.

6. P.L.A.Y. (Pet Lifestyle and You): www.petplay.com
Brand Statement: Luxury designed for pets, people, and the planet.

P.L.A.Y. is a design-led pet brand that promises the world, and delivers. Not just better design, better functionality, and more sustainability – but also great value as they offer a beautiful, functional, high-quality product for much less than other design-led dog bed brands. They claim to "understand the needs of today's Pet Owners" which is evidenced in the superior aesthetics and performance of their products. This is a disruptive brand doing "the same or better, for less" – a very difficult thing to accomplish.

7. BARKBOX: www.barkbox.com
Brand Statement: Make Dogs Happy.

Everything BarkBox does is to make dogs happy. They know that the primary goal of dog parents is to make their kids happy – and that shows up in tons of ways for BarkBox, from the boxes themselves, full of happy-making products, to the Bark Post where they share tons of happy dog stories as well as their live events which they call "pawties." This singular focus will allow BarkBox (who often compare themselves to Disney) to stretch into just about any product, service, or industry as long as it is able to make dogs happy in the process. So no, you won't see any CatBoxes from them... ever.

8. HONEST KITCHEN: www.honestkitchen.com
Brand Statement: Honest to Goodness Foods.

The mission is in the name! Honest kitchen is all about healthy, whole food that is easy to prepare and store. This brand focuses on transparency, its sensational product, and all the benefits associated with it: from animal health and wellness, to the minimal impact on the environment and the positive impact on the family farming industry they buy from. Goodness all around!

9. PET HUB: www.pethub.com
Brand Statement: We Get Lost Pets Home Fast.

PetHub has a very specific mission that is all about protecting pets. Although they are really a tech company, PetHub doesn't focus on "pet technology"; they focus on technology to get lost pets home faster. That's it.

10. HARRY BARKER: www.harrybarker.com
Brand Statement: Because they love us.

This design-led brand leans heavily on the vision and personal brand of its founder, a former model with a remarkable story and impeccable taste. Focused on delivering sensational "beautiful, functional, eco-friendly" products which are "an expression of love" that "bring out what you love most about your dog."

If you visit the websites of these Million Dollar Dog Brands, I guarantee you will see their brand statements there, and more importantly, the site itself, the products, photography, copy, graphics, and colors support what the statement promises 100 per cent.

Lesson: If I were to go to your website right now, would it be crystal clear what you do, and more importantly, WHY you do what you do? No? Your brand statement is the first place to start!

"Be a few people's glass of whiskey, instead of everyone's cup of tea. Don't try to speak to everyone – speak to the people who will be drawn to your personality."

- Jen Caudill

3. Brand Voice

Once you've gone through the exercises to clarify your why, your brand pillars, and your brand statement, it's time to create a formula so from now on, the rest of the wonderful content your brand puts out there sounds exactly the way you want your brand to sound.

This is your chance to have a personality; to prove you're not a robot. This is your golden opportunity to woo potential customers on Twitter in less than 140 characters, to ensure the right people pick your product off the shelf, and to reach those who need you most by speaking directly to them, using their own language.

"After about two-and-a-half years or so, it started to click for us. We like things that are funny and irreverent and when we first started someone actually thought that our company was a media company, like an "I Can Has Cheeseburger" competitor, because of all the funny cat and dog memes we posted in our social media. I thought, that's bad if they thought that is the space that we're in. But when we completely pulled away from our natural personalities and we went with the "protect your pet or they could be lost forever" fear mongering that goes on with pretty much every one of our competitors, people didn't like that either. So what we found was a happy medium for our brand voice." – Lorien, PetHub

"As a company, as a whole, we speak this language very naturally. The hardest part about maintaining that as we grow as a company is the risk of "becoming safe." You don't want to risk everything that you've built and you don't want to offend someone. That starts in the most innocent and well-meaning of ways, so we have worked really, really, really hard to maintain our voice and authenticity and our openness inside the company, and we give everybody the freedom to speak like they speak out in the world.

We don't have strict brand guidelines like, "This is how you must talk and these are the words that you can use." Anyone can pretty much say anything, with the understanding that it's coming from a good place. You know, sometimes we will say offensive things, and sometimes we'll be wrong too; someone will go too far or say the wrong thing. And we'll come in and we'll say, "Well, we apologize for that, we really didn't mean anything by it." But it all comes from people who just really, really mean well and are trying to serve dogs and perform their jobs that way." – Matt, BarkBox

Your brand voice is essentially your brand's way of speaking, the syntax and individual words that your brand uses to communicate its unique personality. Crafting a brand voice is about getting the balance right between personality and structure. It's about knowing the words, feelings and values that your brand stands for so you can wield them easily, with confidence, and passion everywhere you go.

Our delightful copy expert at Working with Dog, Jen Caudill, has passed on some of her suggestions to begin to craft your brand voice:

Points of Difference

The very first tools in your tool box when crafting any copy about what you do as a brand are your points of difference. I suggest focusing on three. Three for your overall brand (these might even be three of your pillars). Once you've outlined what makes your brand unique, it's time to put those points in a list. Not just any list, but a hierarchy; we want to know which point is the most important.

Remember these are points of difference so choosing three that set you apart in the market you're competing in is a good plan.

For instance, if I'm a Natural Dog Treat Co., my hierarchy might be:

- o Healthy
- o Natural
- o Locally-sourced

Once you've got this list, use it as a resource when communicating to your consumers. For example, in a conversation or bit of copy you'd lead with your products being healthy (the point that may be the one most consumers are concerned with), then you'd point out that they're all-natural and then mention that because the ingredients are locally sourced, buying your treats helps family farmers. Boom. You've just made yourself a guide – whether you're chatting in person, writing headlines, social media posts, or About Us information.

Keep the Dogly Principles in Mind:

Be authentic. When you're writing, type as if you're talking to a friend. A great brand voice bucks convention. That may mean starting the occasional sentence with and. And, it may mean a touch of slang, dialect, and one word sentences. Y'all hear what I'm saying? Good.

Be consistent.

I recommend coming up with a list of words and phrases that speak to your brand. Then stick to them. If your products are natural, tasty, and locally-sourced, make sure you've always got those words sprinkled in your messaging. If you've got that brand statement buttoned up, or a killer tagline, use it. This list isn't meant to be all-inclusive (as in, you can never use other words) it's simply meant to make it easier for you when you approach copywriting – so you don't feel the urge to constantly reinvent the wheel. Consistent messaging sticks.

Be clear.

Fancy is just schmancy when it comes to brand messaging. That doesn't mean you can't be elegant. It doesn't mean you can't elevate your brand either, but keep your descriptors and adjectives to a minimum. See the above bullet on consistency. Pick a few and stick to them!

Brand Words

As referenced above, a list of brand words can be a handy tool. Well, two lists actually. One list of words you do use in your brand, and one list of words you do NOT use in your brand. To help with this list, think about where your brand is from regionally. What is the personality you're projecting? What kind of words fit with your brand pillars? What is the personality you want your brand to have: Is it bouncy, fun, and outgoing, or more academic and considered? Is it alternative and edgy, or perhaps sweet and adorable? Infuse as much personality into the "use" list as possible. On the "do not use" list, make sure to list words associated with things you are not cool with, descriptions of dogs or dog owners or your products that drive you nuts when people use them.

Also, consider the opposite personality or price bracket from your brand – what do you not want to be mistaken for? This list will be a helpful guide for you, but especially helpful for on-boarding anyone you hire to help with marketing, copy, or social media work. Obviously other people cannot read your mind so it's good to have some guidelines to help them learn what your brand is all about!

4. Brand Story

For me, one of the great benefits of and motivations for building a Million Dollar Dog Brand is location independence. This is one of my flavors of freedom. In fact, pieces of this book were written in England, Italy, France, Holland, America, and Spain! Last year, my family and I (family is husband and Frenchie = #bromanesupreme on Instagram) had the good fortune to escape to Italy to live for a couple of months.

My mother came to visit us and when she arrived she was determined to find a nice Italian leather journal. We ended up finding a beautiful little market in a lively piazza where a friendly-faced man was selling a selection of leather journals – each with a different design on the cover. He let us browse quietly for a bit, and then as we picked up individual books, he began to explain the origins of the artwork on the covers: explaining the uses for the flower depicted in a 16th century botanical print... sharing the meaning behind the Latin hymn scrawled on an embellished sheet of music... telling us the exact species of fluffy little bird on another, and on and on.

I immediately started sizing him up as a brilliant sales person: He wasn't telling us the facts or figures of how many pages were in the journal or what the paper was made of – he was telling us stories. He was giving each journal a personality. His delivery was compelling and looking around at his leather tools, I wanted to believe that he spends most of his days looking for beautiful and meaningful imagery to imprint into his handmade books and that his life is enriched by the experience.

I realized that even though the stories he told may or may not have been true, I didn't care. I wanted to believe him. I wanted my journal to have a story – and what's more –

I wanted to support him. I wanted to reward him for taking the time to be kind, to tell us stories when he simply could have stood silently or been rude, pushy or super-annoyingly salesy (like many market vendors you often come across in tourist towns). Anyway, I bought one journal and my mom bought three. No doubt we were his ideal customers.

For more about this little experience in Italy (including photos of Charleston our Frenchie traveling around Italy with us) and some great tips on storytelling, check out this article here: workingwithdog.com/3-storytelling/

Lesson: the power of a compelling story of origin. Where the thing comes from, why the thing exists, and what the thing means can totally shift the value of the thing or the level of desire your customer experiences. The efficacy of your story lies in your ability to tap into what your customer wants to believe about herself. In the case of the journal vendor, he was banking on the fact that we didn't want tourist crap; we wanted a real keepsake with some sort of sentimental value. He knew we wanted to believe that we are better buyers than normal tourists because our souvenirs have stories. He was right!

What Should Be in My Origin Story?

There is no right way to tell the story of your brand, but there are a LOT of boring ways! Don't let your story be boring. Give us drama, give us heart, give us humor! Below are some tips for a great brand origin story. You'll see some of the Dogly Principles in there!

Essentially your origin story is all about how your business came to be. Think about some of your favorite brands. Do you know their origin story?

I remember when we started Dog is Good we looked up a great deal to Life is Good, and their "two guys selling tee shirts out of a back of their van" story was so inspiring.

You'll hear several "it all started in my kitchen / living room/ loft/ garage / because my dog" stories from the founders of the Million Dollar Dog Brands in this book. This 'humble beginnings' concept is a great place to start, just don't let it be dull. We want triumph and defeat. We want a hero's journey!

If your story is a bit bland, spice it up with emotional details about what life was like before and what it's like now. Find the drama and puff it up (think reality TV)! Don't forget to consult your points of differentiation and list of brand words for extra inspiration and make sure your why is in there (chances are it will occur naturally in your story). This task is important for your website and sales materials, but you also want to get good at telling it out loud, because as we already know, Million Dollar Dog Brands get a lot of press and one question journalists love to ask is, "How did it all begin?"

How Do I Make My Story Compelling?

1. Engage the senses. Use smells, textures, sights, and sounds of the moments. This will suck our humanity in.

2. Be real: Use real details, be vulnerable, share the loss along with the win, be funny, use real language.

3. Tell an actual STORY: Don't write a bio. Don't be professional; take us on a journey. Have a story arc: a logical start, middle, and end. Bonus points if we fall in love with you along the way (Google "hero's journey" for more detail on how to make that happen).

4. Keep it simple: Don't get too carried away with details that don't matter or with too many descriptive adjectives. Stick to the stuff that moves the story forward (with some nice touches of the sense stuff from #1) and makes you relatable (see #2).

5. Be humble. No one likes a show off. If your business is very successful that's great – and you should definitely say so – but anchor that success with your humble beginnings, your non-stop passion, your learning along the way, and gratitude for customers and colleagues.

Extra credit: Make a video telling the story of your brand. Add imagery and music for extra emotional umph!

Million Dollar Dog Brand Stories

Below are the origin stories of our Million Dollar Dog brands as told to me by the founders. For an interesting comparison, read what they said to me, then have a look at what they say on the "about page" or "our story" page of their website. Which do you find more interesting - the way they told it live in an interview or the way they edited for the site? The lesson here is to infuse more, not less, of your personality and voice into your story. Stop trying to be professional!

Lesson: If I were to go to your website right now, and clicked over to your about page, would I be inspired by what I read? Would I instantly want to meet you or find out more about your products? Would I laugh, cry, feel anything at all?

"It wasn't until I started to get text messages from friends and family with photos of 'Dog is Good' bumper stickers on cars all around the country that I knew our little business had the potential to be something big."

-Nichole, Dog is Good

1. DOG IS GOOD:

My version of the Dog is Good story and how John, Gila and I brought it to life...

When I was young and delightfully naive, I adopted a Great Dane puppy. I was a college student and I happened upon this floppy, spotty, pink-nosed wonder on a sunny Tuesday. There was no plan, and no turning back. She chose me and I was smart enough to say yes. Everything changed after that, and inspired by my new love I started a pet photography business (this was back in 2005 before pet photography was really a thing). We lived in a super small town where we met Gila Kurtz, a local dog trainer. I photographed her and her dogs and we signed up for one of her training classes and we became friends. She and her husband John had this idea. They saw an opportunity in the pet industry to make tee shirts and other goods for dog lovers; stuff that was clever and much cooler than big boxy tee-shirts with breed-specific watercolor portraits on them. All of us wanted to make something that really expressed what it is to share a life with dog - the good, the bad, and the hilariously inappropriate. Plus, they had a great name: Dog is Good. I was sold. As a photographer and graphic artist, I spent most of my time working with the intangible and I loved the idea of being able to make something real – something I could hold and see on shelves and proudly say, I made that! So, we joined forces and set about to bring this idea to life.

Not long after, the Kurtzes moved to Southern California. Before they left, I threw together a simple 'dog is good' word mark using a typewriter font (which is still one of my favorite DIG designs) and we had it embroidered on a bunch of hats and visors. After diving headlong into the weird world of screen printing, we also found our way to getting our first few tee shirts made. Gila sold those early samples so quickly that we knew it was time to get serious. So I scheduled a trip down to CA with the goal of creating a "proper brand." Something epic. Something iconic. Something every dog lover would want. Easier said than done! For days I toiled over my sketchbook. Poured through anything I could get my hands on that might inspire me. Nothing. Then, in a moment of strange coincidence, our beloved "Bolo" logo finally came to us. I mocked up our first simple website with flat illustrations of a light blue sky, puffy white clouds, and our tee-shirts hanging on a clothes line, we settled on the tagline "inspired by Dog" and that was that. The Dog is Good brand was born. We chose a handful of our favorite product ideas (we had way more ideas than we could make all at once) and I began mocking them up. We all researched how and where to have them made and who we might sell them to. The Kurtzes' living room became DIG HQ. But it wasn't until I started to get emails and text messages from friends and family sending me photos of Dog is Good bumper stickers on cars all around the country that I knew our little business had the potential to be something big.

"L.L. Bean came by and ordered 8,000 bowls. We were off and running... they placed orders for 8,000 bowls every month for the next year and then ramped up from there."

– Patrick, Ruffwear

2. RUFFWEAR:

I have been a long-time admirer of the Ruffwear brand. They have always just been so clear about what they do and who they're for. You know when you buy a Ruffwear product that it's going to do the job and it's going to last. I was thrilled to catch up with Patrick between his outdoor adventures to find out more about his Million Dollar Dog Brand:

Patrick: "You know, there really wasn't a big picture. The idea came out of just a whimsical day out on a mountain bike ride. We had joined a couple friends up in Los Padres National Forest in Southern California. We were out for a mountain bike ride, and two of the folks that we were with are engineers and very thoughtful folks, and they had thought ahead and brought along a plastic bag and some water to water their dog with. After we had been riding for a while, we stopped and we all took a little break. Liz had thoughtfully brought this bag, and she offered the bag full of water to her dog, and her dog Mochi came over and investigated the bag, stuck his nose in it, and then promptly walked away.

Basically, she was left holding the bag, and she couldn't set it down, she couldn't pour it back in her bottle. Water was a scarce commodity because we were out in the backcountry, and we had to carry everything in with us. So, she turned to me and said, "Hey, you need to come up with a solution for this." I kind of joked and laughed, and said, "Why me?" On the way home, when we were driving back about 70 miles south, I started thinking, if we have waterproof fabrics, and we can keep water from coming and getting us wet, why can't we turn that inside out and just keep water in?

At the time, I already had a company called Salamander Paddle Gear. We made a bunch of paddle sports equipment, so I was involved in a whole cut and sew operation. So I just took some of our existing technical fabrics and made a quick mock-up with one of our sample sewers. The first one worked pretty well – it was basically a collapsible food and water bowl. I set this thing in our back yard with our two dogs and was just kind of experimenting with it, seeing how long it would last, what the sun would do to it. How long would it hold water? It was really a curiosity for me.

The amazing thing about that prototype was that everyone who came over looked at it, and you could almost see the light bulb coming on over their head. They would see this thing and go, "What is this thing? How does it do that?". That's basically what our first product was, the collapsible food and water bowl. I ended up making another 15 of them and kind of refining the pattern a little bit. I took it to an outdoor retailer show,

I think this was back in about '94, and put it alongside Salamander Paddle gear on this little card table. I had come up with this logo and little tagline: "Gear for the dogs on the go." Everybody would come by, and their focus would turn to this bowl. It turns out that during that visit, L.L. Bean came by and became very interested in it, and then subsequently ordered 8,000 bowls from us. They placed orders for 8,000 bowls every month for the next year."

"I was straight out of school, broke, and I had no idea how I was going to do it, I just had this feeling. I just knew that this would be big one day if I really pursued it."

-Thadeu, Zee.Dog

3. ZEE.DOG:

I absolutely loved chatting with Thadeu, co-founder of Zee.Dog (you can call him Thad). He is full of great energy and is delightful to know. I found his story super inspiring. I hope you do too. He is all hustle, no excuses:

Thad: "It was back in 2009 when I lived in LA, right next to UCLA. I've had dogs all my life and when I was in LA, it was the first time that I was living by myself. I needed a dog in my life. Energetically, I just always need one beside me. So I decided to adopt one and his name was Zeca. This was the first time that I was going out looking for products for a dog; in the past my mom had been the one buying. As I shopped around, I realized that there were a ton of options, but nothing that I wanted. There wasn't really a brand that sort of stood out from the crowd. You know, if you're going to Petco or PetSmart, you just see hundreds and thousands of products but it seemed like there was nobody paying attention to details. There was nobody really doing a lot of great branding.

At the time, there was this famous brand called Skull Candy, you know, they're known for headphones. They revolutionized the headphone industry by creating a brand with a statement around the product, right? So it wasn't just grey headphones anymore. They were putting prints and colors and they were creating a community that people wanted to be a part of. So I was like, I think there's an opportunity here like Skull Candy in the pet industry. But I was straight out of school, broke, and I had no idea how I was going to do it – I just had this feeling. I just knew that this would be big one day if I really pursued it. So, I moved back in with my twin brother and we started working on Zee.Dog – initially just concepts and names and logos. We had a clear idea of what we wanted to do but it was just going to be a long road. We knew we needed big funding, so that we could produce stuff in mass quantities and really scale. We didn't want to launch small because we knew it would be eaten up by somebody who looked and it and said, "Wow this is a good idea." So it took us almost three years, from concept to going over to China, creating prototypes and then sitting down with investors. It was basically three years from idea to getting funded and then eventually launching in 2012. But our very first pre-seed funding was actually on Kick Starter. We were actually the first Brazilian guys on Kick Starter. They were really early on too. At the time, raising $10,000 on Kick Starter was huge. We needed $10,000 to fly over to China and create prototypes. My brother just got on the plane and it was really an adventure. The language barrier was crazy, he didn't know anybody. Today, that same person that picked him up at the airport back then is now our China Operations Manager and she now runs 15 of our factories in China. We've grown a lot in these last years. We had a lot of people saying, "You guys are crazy." There were even a lot of investors saying, "You know, you should be doing tech, everybody's investing in tech. What are you doing in consumer goods? What are you doing in the pet industry?" We eventually got funded in 2012 and then we just started growing like crazy, so it's been a fun ride."

"We wanted the be the pioneers, creating products that were 100% socially responsible: from the material, to the way they are made to the way that they are packaged, so that's what we did."

-Stephanie, Planet Dog

4. PLANET DOG:

Planet Dog is easily one of the great pioneering Million Dollar Dog Brands. Since 1997 (that's 20 years you guys) they have been living their core values and making great, innovative, and fun stuff for dogs. It was great to catch up with Stephanie, who is as warm and delightful as people get, to have her share their story:

Nichole: "So wind back a little bit. You were named by Fast Company as one of the Fast 50, one of the most innovative companies. And that was in 2003, that was 13 years ago. That was a lifetime ago! In the interview you said that Planet Dog was founded by two Ben-and-Jerry's-eating, Patagonia-wearing guys who happened to love their dogs like family. I thought that was brilliant. And your tagline at that time was to "Amuse, Explore, Innovate, Create, Philanthropate, and Celebrate - all in the name of the dog." So, fill us in, back to where you started and then where are you guys now?"

Stephanie: "Sure, great question. Wow, that brings back a lot of amazing memories.

I think they are something to reflect on and be really proud of! Alex and Stew, who are the two guys that I'm talking about in the article, and although I was a partner to them at the time, I came on board more as a friend, rather than a partner partner. We only had, I guess you could say, four-legged kids. They were everything to us.

They talked about a lot of ideas to start. They knew that they wanted to be a values-led and driven company; that meant everything to them, similar to Patagonia and Ben and Jerry's, where they gave back to community and they knew that they wanted to make a great product. They didn't know how, they didn't know when, they didn't know what they were going to do, and as we were sitting there with our dogs at our feet, that is how it came about. Literally, we were sitting there looking at our dogs and we said, "It's gotta be for our dogs." Back then it just didn't exist in the pet industry, like not at all. This was in 1997. So, we did a lot of research. Ironically not in the pet industry at first, but in other multi-channel, like-minded, values-driven brands like Stonyfield Farm, Ben and Jerry's, Patagonia, and at the time, Smith & Hawken was a company that we really embraced.

We went to go see Gary Hirshberg, who was the founder of Stonyfield Farm, and he inspired us and motivated us and we knew that's that what we really were going to do. We did some research in the pet industry and saw that there weren't many companies that were multi-channel. What I mean by that is not only selling to the end consumers, but to other retailers as well. So we did it. We wanted the be the pioneers, if you will, in creating products that were socially responsible. 100% socially responsible. From the material, to the way that they are made and the way that they are packaged, and that's how we launched. We launched with exactly sixteen SKUs, and they consisted of hemp and fleece that were made out of recycled soda bottles. We made collars, leashes, toys, beds, feedbags, and travel bowls. That's how Planet Dog started!"

"That was it. I became fascinated with dog behavior. The question I was asking myself was, how can two predatory species live together so successfully? I've been trying to discover the answer to that question ever since."

-Victoria Stilwell

5. VICTORIA STILWELL:

Interviewing Victoria for this book was great fun because we got to dive into topics that she normally doesn't get asked about as a dog trainer, advocate, and influencer. I've included her in this book, not because she's trying to earn millions, that's not her motivation at all, but because along the way she has built a powerful brand that fights for dogs. She is a great example of how and why to build a Million Dollar Dog Brand, even if all you want to do is change the world.

Victoria: I've always been an entrepreneur and I've always loved animals. When I was at university, you know, you've got to earn some cash, so I'd started these businesses everywhere. One of the businesses I remember was one of my friends and I decided we would make sandwiches in Enfield, which is in north London.

We thought we'd make sandwiches and go down to Camden Market and sell them to make some cash, and so we did, and we actually made quite a bit of money. We were in our early twenties and we had no idea you needed to have a food license! I was always looking for new ideas, new ways to create a business. After university I went to drama school because I wanted to be an actor and it was at drama school that I carried on with a job that I'd kind of been doing throughout university and drama school. That was dog sitting. It was through dog sitting that I became a dog walker, and I remember I was walking one dog a day and by the end of the month, because of word of mouth, I was walking 20 dogs a day! I found that not only was I earning a lot of money, but I was also loving what I was doing. In fact, the money sort of ceased to be important. It was great to pay the rent, but it ceased to be the most important thing. The fact that I was getting out and I was bringing some joy into these dogs' lives every day while their owners were at work, and the freedom that I felt walking these animals, it just felt right. One day when I was walking at Wimbledon Common, a guy came up to me who was a trainer, and he asked me, "Do your dogs ever fight?" and I said, "No!" he asked, "Do your dogs ever run away?" I said, "No!" Now remember, I'm walking 20 a day, so 10 in the morning, 10 in the afternoon, and they're all off-leash, by the way, they're all off the leash. In Wimbledon Common you could do that then. I said, "No!" and he said, "Have you ever wondered why?" and I said "No!" and he said, "Do you want to find out?"

Nichole: What a great sales pitch!

Victoria: Yes! It's a great sales pitch! And that was it. From there I learned so much, and I started going to lectures, reading, and studying. I became fascinated with dog behavior. The question I was asking myself was how can two predatory species live together so successfully? I've been trying to discover the answer to that question ever since."

"When I saw how much my wife spent on Momo, I started to look into the pet industry and I realized, whoa! We're not alone, a lot of Pet Parents actually spend a lot on their pets – there's definitely an opportunity there if there's a good idea."

-Will, P.L.A.Y.

6. P.L.A.Y. (Pet Lifestyle and You)
Will Chen is one of my favorite petpreneurs. He is one of the most intelligent, hardest working people I know. It was an honor for me to be there at the beginning to watch P.L.A.Y come to life. Here's what Will had to say about the origins of P.L.A.Y:

Will: "I think for most entrepreneurs in the pet industry it's a very common theme, a very common storyline for how we start building businesses. We are all passionate pet lovers and one way or another we all start our businesses because of the pets around us, in our case it's no different. Back in 2009, my wife and I had our first dog, a pug named Momo. We were in a time of transition in our lives.

I was a management consultant, my wife was working in the finance industry. She went back to school and it was a pretty tough period because of the financial crisis. I was flying every week and so having a dog at home really just changed our life up in a really positive way.

Actually, a funny story, was that one of the beds we got from one of the mass retail chains, we brought it home and Momo just treated it like a pee pad – we still joke about it – she just peed on it, like she thought, "This is far too poor to be my bed, I think I'll use it as a potty." So we had to toss it out! It only cost $30, but to toss out $30 within a day of buying it, I felt like, "great, there goes more money out the window." As we started to buy things like this for Momo I realized that well-designed products were super pricey and mass-market products in chains were typically not that high in quality. There didn't seem to be a middle ground. When I saw how much my wife spent on Momo, I started to look into the pet industry and I realized, whoa! We're not alone, a lot of Pet Parents actually spend a lot on their pets – there's definitely an opportunity there if there's a good idea.

At the same time, I was looking into the next step in my career, so the timing just kind of naturally worked out. I left my firm, and I went to Berkeley to do a year of classes in finance, which is when I met a lot of designer friends here in the Bay Area, and also met you, Nichole, through a photoshoot we did with our puppy, Momo. So, your story with Dog is Good and the influence of friends like you led me to thinking whether there is an interesting opportunity in there. The last piece of the puzzle is that I come from a family with a manufacturing background. So, it helps to have expertise and leverage with my parents who can advise me on the production side of things, and when I was building the business model, their input and also their mentorship was very useful. Those were the pieces that allowed us to get started."

"I wanted to surprise my dog all the time and the options were pretty poor. Pretty much every day I came home with a $10 bully stick. He was fine with that, I think he was pretty happy with it actually, but I was disappointed. I wanted to discover cool new things for him all the time, and I wasn't finding a way to do that."

-Matt, BarkBox

7. BARKBOX:

Matt and I have something in common, and that is the love of a Great Dane. His boy's name is Hugo and he's the reason BarkBox exists. Matt, co-founder of BarkBox, tells us about Hugo and how the phenomenon that is BarkBox began:

Matt: "Hugo's my boy. He is almost six, he's my baby. I'm obsessed with him. He's a mantle Great Dane. He is very handsome, but I think he knows it. He's very friendly, he loves all other dogs, and just wants to be friends with all of them. He's just the best boy ever. He has just had an effect on me that I think is probably familiar to people who have children, which is, you know, you want the all best for that baby.

You want to make them happy, you want to make them as healthy as possible. So probably, three out of five days a week, as I'd come home from work I'd stop in to a pet store and asked what they had for my dog? I'd say, "He's a Great Dane, he's growing really quickly, what do you have? Is there a new toy?" I wanted to surprise him all the time, and the options were pretty poor. Pretty much every day I came home with a $10 bully stick. And he was fine with that. I think he was pretty happy with it actually, but I was disappointed. I wanted to discover cool new things for him all the time, and I wasn't finding a way to do that.

From there was born the idea of BarkBox: We can send you a package of toys and treats and things that make your dog really happy, personalized especially for your dog. If it's a big Great Dane who plays in a certain way, then we'll get the right products for that dog, and if it's a small Chihuahua who doesn't really like toys but loves treats, we satisfy that dog too. Prior to BarkBox, I started Meetup.com, which is also a subscription business. So I loved the subscription model, I knew a lot about what worked already, and that's how we got going."

"I started a homemade raw food diet for him using my own ingredients. I got incredible results. I cured his ear infections and managed to destroy my kitchen in the process: bowls of bloody meat in the fridge and spinach up the walls!"

- Lucy, Honest Kitchen

8. HONEST KITCHEN

I was thrilled to get a chance to chat with Lucy, founder of Honest Kitchen. It's so exciting to talk to an entrepreneur braving the ridiculously giant brand-dominated and competitive pet food space. Here's what she had to say:

Lucy: "It actually started in my own kitchen, back in 2002. I had a Rhodesian Ridgeback named Mosey at the time, and was dealing with some chronic ongoing ear infections that just kept on flaring up, despite all of the medications and other treatments I was getting from the vet. I was doing ear flushes and antibiotics and all of those fun things, and it would kind of subside and suppress the symptoms and then just keep on flaring up.
So I ended up thinking, maybe his food could be causing his problems and perhaps food could be his medicine as well.

So, I started basically a homemade raw food diet for him just using my own ingredients and ended up actually getting incredible results. I cured his ear infections and managed to destroy my kitchen in the process! The bowls of bloody meat in the fridge and spinach up the walls and things didn't go down too well. I finally found dehydration as a perfect way to continue feeding him a healthy, colorful, whole food diet, without all of the mess. Just removing the moisture, which is really what makes raw so messy, and making it into a dehydrated, shelf-stable product that I could just serve as needed. There really wasn't anything like it on the market at the time in the terms of a commercial product, so I thought well, maybe I could sort of make it into a little business.

I connected with suppliers of dehydrated foods. A number of them actually took quite a bit of battling via telephone to even persuade them to sell their ingredients to me. This whole concept of being "human grade for pets" was a bit baffling to some of the perspective suppliers, so it took a bit of persuading to actually let me buy their ingredients for use in a pet food product. They didn't really want their ingredients being associated with pet foods, but that was really my biggest kind of mandate for the product, was to have a finished food that was 100% human food grade. Now we actually have a statement of no objection from the federal FDA to use the term "human grade" on our labeling because every single ingredient that we source is directly from the human food supply chain. So, it was really just working with suppliers and then putting together my own blends of ingredients, working with a lot of spreadsheets to calculate the nutritional profiles of the finished recipes and then obviously, Mosey has to give the final paw of approval."

"Only 25% of pets that go into shelters get home again. It's less than 2% for cats! He said, 'This is ridiculous, I've got to do something!' *So he started PetHub.*"

-Lorien, PetHub

9. PETHUB:

To tell PetHub's story I chose to chat with the incredible Lorien Clemens, PetHub's Director of Marketing. She has been with PetHub since very early days and she had tons of insights to share about how they've built a Million Dollar Dog Brand in pet tech way before pet tech was a trend:

Lorien: "Our founder and CEO, Tom Arnold, left Microsoft because he felt the need to make a difference, a profound difference.

Something that he could tangibly feel, rather than working at the back offices or Microsoft running a team that nobody had ever heard of. Inspired by his pets, he began looking for areas where he could apply his tech background in the pet industry. He found that the technology that was being used to get lost pets home was by and large still stuck in the 18th century, when the ID tag for a dog was first invented. Put in your dog's name and how to reach you in some way.

Though microchips had certainly helped, it clearly had not solved the problem when you have half the pets that enter shelters not going out again. Only 25% of pets that go into shelters go home again to their owners. That's for dogs and it's less than 2% for cats! So, he said, "This is ridiculous, I've got to do something!" So he started PetHub, which in essence is a digital ID tag that links to an online profile and now an entire suite, and that's where our story began."

"I love to sew, I had a lot of time on my hands and a lot of textiles stashed away. So, I just started making stuff for dogs and giving them as gifts... I would give them a bed, a robe, and a towel and they were just blown away by it."

-Carol, Harry Barker

10. HARRY BARKER

When founder Carol told this story to me it was immediately one of my favorites. It's funny, weird and awesome (see how much personality is in here! Be more like Carol - be brave enough to be like this on your website!)

Carol: "Well, I started Harry Barker on my kitchen table with two sewing machines and a pair of hands in Manhattan. I had a loft in Chelsea and I was homebound and unemployed because I had Cushing's disease (I actually didn't know yet that I had Cushing's disease). I didn't know what to do with myself because I was a former fashion model; I was a Victoria's Secret model, I modeled for Vogue and did every designer and every major fashion brand.

I thought I hit the lottery on having been lucky enough to be born to work as a professional model. But then I turned thirty, which is ancient – that's like dog years in modelling, way too old. So, I started fire-eating with Penn & Teller...

Nichole: I'm sorry, you what?

Carol: I was a fire-eater. I just wanted to get all that out of the way. I was a fashion model, a Victoria's Secret model and a fire-eater.

Nichole: I love that you just throw that out there, like I was a fire-eater.

Carol: When I was 34, 35, Penn & Teller moved to Las Vegas and I got really sick and I started gaining a lot of weight. I gained almost 60 pounds over about eight months and went to every doctor I could find. In New York City, I had all the best doctors and nobody knew what was wrong with me. I kept gaining more weight, and had a hump, and a beard and my hair started falling out and I just transformed. I became this other person. I was trapped inside this body that wasn't mine. I started pet-sitting in my loft. I really couldn't go out much so I just started dog-sitting and watching peoples' dogs when they went on vacation and knitting dog sweaters and making doggy bathrobes and baking doggy biscuits. I loved to sew and I'm crafty, and I had a lot of time on my hands and a lot of textiles stashed away. So, I just started making stuff for dogs and giving them as gifts to people who would return from their vacations. I would return their dog and give them a bed and a robe and a towel and they were just blown away by it. They loved it, they hadn't seen anything like it. I'd color coordinate it for their loft or their apartment because these were friends of mine, so it looked really nice in their home.

They didn't have to shove the dog bed in the closet when company would come because they were embarrassed by it. Anyways, it just seemed logical. And then an editor saw it in somebody's loft and said, "Oh that's so pretty, let's photograph it for InStyle - and that's where Harry Barker began!"

Give yourself a treat!

You're now through sense 1 - the most difficult, mind-bending part of this book! Hopefully you are well on your way to understanding and creating your four "why tools": your Brand Pillars, Brand Statement, Brand Voice, and Brand Story. Be patient, I cannot emphasize enough that this is a process and it takes time. I describe this to my clients as "percolating" – you need to start the process and then let it bubble away, little by little in the background as you watch the pieces slowly pull together.

Clarity will emerge, don't force it. Don't rush it. Great brands are always working on this stuff, revising it, letting their customers influence their identity and staying flexible to meet the future, so don't think you're going to write this stuff in stone, ever. Just start at the beginning. Acknowledge the value in the process, and begin it!

14. Sense Two: Sense of Sight

Now that we have tackled our first, very essential marketing sense, our "why," we are now on to the second of our marketing senses, our Sense of Sight: our "who."

What is It?

The second of the Marketing Senses, the Sense of Sight, involves taking your first sense, your new message around "why you do what you do," and look around to see who also believes what you believe. Who is it that you are most suited to serve based on everything you've outlined in your brand pillars? This sense is your "who" sense.

Why Does it Matter?

I think we can all agree that knowing who your customers are is incredibly helpful. How can you sell to someone if you don't know who they are? But it involves more than just slapping some demographic data down like "our customers are affluent, educated women 25-65" or "DINKs (Dual Income No Kids)" or "Empty Nesters," in order to connect with our audience emotionally.

We need some emotional data. We need to know what our customers fear, what they desire, what they stress over on a daily basis, and what they want other people to believe about them. These are the critical data points that matter to brands. These are your tools for building "know, like and trust." These are your keys to the doors into their world, their heart, and their wallet. Think of this process as finding common ground with your ideal client, people who will be able to see what they want to believe about themselves in your brand.

We agreed at the beginning of this book that our reason for investing in building a brand is to make more money. We agreed that a brand is the best vehicle to connect emotionally with our customers so we can have greater influence over their behavior, thus allowing us to create more or higher-value transactions. This "connecting emotionally" process starts by knowing who "they" are and what they want, think, and feel. Once we know this, we can craft communications that speak to those desires, thoughts, stresses, and feelings very, very specifically.

"We have built a brand that our people want to be part of. Our fans, don't have just one collar. I've seen people send emails to the company who have every single collar we've made since we launched. They have more prints than we actually have. They collect and keep them in the packaging... they have two or three of each design just in case one gets broken! They're fanatics and we love them. They are why we do what we do." – Thad, Zee.Dog

How Does it Show Up?

When we were discussing "brand voice" a few pages ago, Jen said, "Be a few people's glass of whiskey, instead of everyone's cup of tea. Don't try to speak to EVERYONE – speak to the people who will be drawn to your personality." Remember that?

This is another place (like leading with the why, instead of the what) where we have go against our natural instincts. Most of us find it VERY uncomfortable to be specific, to use targeted language, to risk alienating people, because we live in fear of not having enough customers.

Example: Do you call yourself a "pet business" or call your customers "Pet Parents" even though you work almost exclusively with dogs? Does the language on your website reflect this, using the word "pet" instead of "dog"? Is this because you don't want to turn off the 2% of cat owners who use your business? What would happen if you became a business just for dogs and spoke only to dog owners? Something to think about!

Here's the thing, most of us Pet Parents don't identify with having "pets." I certainly don't, I have a dog. His name is Charlie, and his role in my life is more like that of human child than whatever role a "pet" is supposed to have. I don't consider him a "pet" and I am not drawn to products or services with images of generic paw print pet art or cats because I don't have a generic pet or a cat. I have a dog. I am a dog parent. I am Charlie's parent. He has name and a whole list of personality quirks, physical conditions, unique dietary needs, and funny habits. Our daily life and my purchasing decisions are driven by that stuff. THAT is the stuff you need to be talking about, showing me photos of and discussing in your marketing so I know you get it. You get him, you get our relationship. So I know your products or services will meet my very high expectations.

This "who" sense shows up in your ability to be brave enough to speak only to those customers who you actually want and you are ideally positioned to serve best. The ones you actually understand. Feel free to alienate everyone else – let them go – they don't matter to you. If you're trying to sell to me, you have to master the art of speaking to me about my ridiculous seven-year-old Frenchie, not about my pet.

Get this right, and I will stay with you forever, all the while spending heavily, thus negating those three generic Pet Owners who bought one thing from you one time.

How to Master the "Who" Sense

Don't worry. I know what I just explained is not an easy thing to do. It's not simple to talk to 10,000 people and make each one of them feel like you're talking to them about their exact critter. It's not simple, but it is possible. It all starts with knowing what role they feel they play in their pet's life.

Oh, I know who my clients are, they're "Pet Parents."
Before we work together I always ask my clients who their ideal client is and more often than not, somewhere in that answer are the words 'Pet Parent." Are these words you use to describe your ideal customer? Let's explore who a Pet Parent really is, shall we?

A Framework for Understanding Pet Parents

It's no secret that the role of dogs and cats in many Western homes has been evolving from that of a household pet to that of a child. Retail expert Phil Chang from Hubba.com confirms the trend, saying "Studies have shown that when humans look at their pets, they feel the same emotional affinity as they do when they look at their children. In fact, nine in 10 Americans say they consider their pet to be a part of their family.

Furthermore, the average number of dogs per household worldwide is 1.6, while cats are 2.1. The average number of children per household worldwide is 2. While the number of children per household has remained stagnant, pet ownership has tripled in the United States since the 1970s." It seems many couples worldwide are literally choosing to have dogs and cats in their life and home instead of children, so the term "Pet Parent" seems natural. Simultaneously, the term "Pet Owner," and in fact the entire legal and moral idea that a pet is piece of property, has been widely rejected by Pet Guardians who know their companions to be complex sentient beings and not "things."

For those of us who operate pet businesses and target this broad, ambiguous market called "Pet Parents," the real question is: Who are they? Furthermore, what motivates them? Additionally, based on your unique business model, brand, skills, and capabilities, are they in fact your ideal customer?

Human Hierarchy of Needs

So it's likely that you will have heard of Maslow's Hierarchy of Needs, but in case you're not familiar, this pyramid-shaped diagram outlines Maslow's theory, that we as humans move up a specific process of need satisfaction.

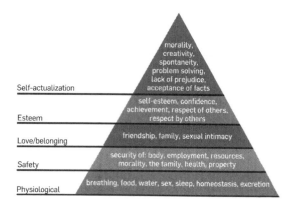

Basically as our basic needs are met (food, water, shelter), we have the capacity to care about and pursue higher and higher (less survival-related) needs. This theory has received criticism, largely for lack of empirical support and inherent cultural bias, but I think it's an interesting framework to use to try to piece together these Pet Parent questions.

Pet Hierarchy of Roles

I would like to propose a theory about the Pet Parent identity as it relates to our businesses' ability to profit and grow. The concept we will explore here is the idea that there is a hierarchy that exists in the roles pets occupy in our lives; thus, in the human role as a pet caretaker. Additionally, that this hierarchy can be broken down into three distinct levels, each presenting unique opportunities for pet businesses to serve, problem solve, and profit from. In other words, below is a model to help determine if your customers are in fact Pet Parents and if so, how you can best serve them.

As previously discussed, pets cannot fulfil their own needs. Therefore, unlike Maslow's pyramid, which identifies human needs and the ascension of a human up the pyramid as they become more capable and interested in pursuing their greatest potential as a human being, we will identify pets' needs, and the ascension of the human up the pyramid as they become more capable and interested in pursuing their greatest potential as a caretaker of pets. So we've got a pyramid of pet needs and three basic levels of how well their human caretakers are meeting those needs. Make sense?

For our purposes, we have borrowed Maslow's categories, changing "self-actualization" to "enrichment," and combined them into three distinct levels:

Roles of Pets and Their Caretakers

1. **Pet Owner** (Pets as Property)
2. **Pet Guardian** (Pets as Sentient)
3. **Pet Parent** (Pets as Kids)

Pet Hierarchy of Roles Pyramid

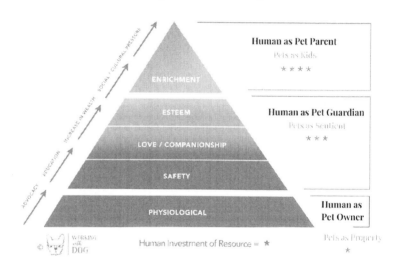

1. Pet Owner: Pets as Property

This is the very base level of pet caretaking. Varying from pets as an acceptable food source or commodity, to pets that live without shelter year-round with only base needs met, to working animals that are considered valuable only as long as their utility lasts. At this level the pet is essentially a thing, not a who. In most cases the bare minimum of time and money are invested in the animals' care.

Primary Sales Opportunity: Low Cost

Due to the minimal investment of resources in pets as property, it is likely that the best strategy to attract buyers at the Pet Owner level is to offer low price and high convenience.

2. Pet Guardian: Pets as Sentient

Pet Owners become Pet Guardians as the animals' safety and emotional wellbeing become a greater concern. The fundamental difference between "Pets as Property" and "Pets as Sentient" is the human's acknowledgment that the animal is not a thing but a sentient being with thoughts and feelings. For dogs and cats, this often leads to the animal moving inside to share the home, which then leads to an increase in behavior and cleanliness-related problems to solve. Additionally, as the human acknowledges that the animal has thoughts and feelings, a greater bond can form which leads to love and belonging, thus the pet may start to be considered 'family." This level is the beginning of a better understanding of the pets' needs for grooming, nutrition, exercise, and quality of life. In most developed Western cultures, the mass market would fall in this Pet Guardian Category and many pet caretakers who fall into this category may consider themselves "Pet Parents."

Primary Sales Opportunity: Solve Problems

Due to the integration of the pet into the human home, we propose that best strategy to attract buyers at the pet guardian level is to seek to solve their basic behavior and co-habitation annoyances. There is an increase of time and financial resources available at this level, but due to the limited nature of those resources, great value and convenience will be very important factors to influence purchases.

Sample Problems Solving Products and Topics:

- ○ Loose-leash walking
- ○ Containment (crates, fences, doors)
- ○ Barking
- ○ Odors and stains
- ○ Basic supplies and accessories
- ○ Basic training tools
- ○ Chewing
- ○ Grooming
- ○ Diet: Basic nutrition, allergies, weight Loss, illness
- ○ Masstige gifts / items for Pet Parents and the home

3. Pet Parent: Pets as Kids

The fundamental difference between a Pet Guardian and a Pet Parent is that the human's acknowledgement of sentience becomes a more comprehensive concern with holistic health, wellbeing, enrichment, happiness, and force-free training methods. Pet parents feel compelled to make the very best decisions they can for their companion. Consequently, Pet Parents invest a great deal of resources in learning about and acting upon their pets' unique, instinctual, emotional, and cognitive needs.

In consumer cultures like America, this powerful emotional need to act in the animal's best interest often outweighs the practical considerations of cost and convenience, leading to Pet Parents representing both a very profitable and a very educated segment of the market. This commitment to deeply understanding and acting on their pets' highest needs is the realization of a human's highest potential as a caretaker of animals. By these definitions, despite whether they think of themselves as a Pet Parent, a pet caretaker is not at this level without making these significant commitments to truly understanding their companion animal(s).

Primary Retail Opportunity: Enrichment

The Pet Guardian becomes the Pet Parent as they begin to treat the needs of their pet like they would the needs of a child. At this level, the Pet Parent often shows love through the investments of time and money in their animals' wellbeing so there are significant opportunities here to find and keep customers with incredibly high lifetime value.

Along with the increased spending, however, comes high expectations, so the ability to increase conversions among these consumers is largely impacted by the quality of your offering and the ability of you and/or your staff to offer sound, specialist advice. It is likely that exceeding the customers' expectations with service-oriented extras will be rewarded with loyalty.

It is important to remember, however, that just like all humans, Pet Parents still want and need good value. So don't make the mistake of simply thinking high-priced "luxury" offerings will unanimously appeal to buyers at this level.

Sample Enrichment Categories and Topics:

- Force-free training tools and resources*
  *Additionally this passionate, educated consumer will expect a total absence of force or pain-causing training philosophies and tools: no pinch, no choke, no prong!
- Natural and Holistic Wellness
- Grain-free, single-ingredient, home-cooked diets
- RAW or BARF diets
- Dietary supplements
- Organic / local products
- Enrichment toys and activities
- Premium supplies and accessories
- Design-led brands
- Premium gifts / items for Pet Parents

- ○ Premium pet-themed or "designed with pet in mind" home goods
- ○ Advanced problem solvers (Catios, toys for heavy chewers, advanced health services, allergies)

So What Does This All Mean?

The importance of all of this relates directly to your ability to define your "who" so you can find them and influence their behavior (a.k.a. get them to buy from you, tell a friend, and buy again)! The first step as you look at this pyramid is to determine who you feel most inclined to serve. More importantly, who are you most well-suited to serve?

Do you look for good value above all things? Are you interested in having a high-volume business or brand? Would selling into Walmart be a dream come true? Pet Owners and budget-conscious Pet Guardians are your "who."

Do you want to make something really great but still affordable and hope to get into PetCo or PetSmart one day? Are you interested in offering a service that many people know they need (sitting, grooming, walking)? Do you want to solve one or more of the basic problems that pet caretakers who share their home with their pets have? (See the list above.) Then Pet Guardians are most likely your ideal market. If you're in America, Canada, UK, or Australia, it is likely that the Pet Guardian market is the largest audience, so it certainly is a strong place to position your brand. It's possible Pet Parents will be interested in your brand too, but they won't be your primary target.

Do you specialize in a small niche within animal wellbeing? Are you obsessed with providing the highest possible quality service or product? Are you interested in working with highly educated, discerning pet caretakers? Are you passionate about force-free training methods? Are you fascinated by canine or feline cognition and very interested in the enrichment needs of pets?
Then you are perfectly suited to serve the Pet Parent market. If you're working with this growing space within the pet industry, you are going to have to BRING it on all levels: quality, transparency, practicality, design, function, and purpose. This consumer really cares why you do what you do – because they are taking your philosophy into consideration when they purchase from you.

The second step is to take note of the opportunities outlined above for the pet role you intend to serve and keep them in mind as we move on to the next exercise.

HINT: Since we're not getting into the other Marketing Stages in this book, I just want to share a helpful tip for stages two to four. From now on, consider tailoring your blogs, emails, signage, promotions, social media posts, and other marketing communications to speak directly and specifically to what you know about the realities of your Pet Owner, Pet Guardian and/or Pet Parent customers.

This is a shortcut to that difficult task of talking to 10,000 people and making each one of them feel like you're talking to them about their pet.

Pet Parent Map

The next step in our "who" discovery, is to take what you now know about your ideal customer, based on whether they are a Pet Owner, Pet Guardian or Pet Parent, and start to create some individual people or "avatars" that represent our exact people so that we know how to speak to them.

The first question to think about is if you own a dog or a cat, does that define you? No, not for most people.

You might also be a pilot or a physicist, a wife or a sister, an expert chess player or an avid Seahawks fan. (Shout out to Seattle, my home-town!) The bottom line is that we need to know more about our ideal client than the simple fact that they care for a pet and as discussed above, we certainly need to know what KIND of pet because using the word "pet" is not the way to go when trying to connect!

Starting with the most fundamental and working towards the more detailed, we need to create a story about our ideal client. A story based on facts based on research and customer data and a bit of improvisation based on what we know about people who believe what we believe. Plus of course, we can add in details based on what we think we know about our person based on whether they are a Pet Owner or a Pet Guardian or a Pet Parent.

We want to know our ideal client like a dear friend so we can speak to her like one... Not just by using the word Pet Parent (a term she may or may not even connect with – nobody likes to feel like a statistic or a marketing segment). This is why research and insights are so important.

Ideal Client Map

At Working with Dog we use a tool called the "ideal client map." You can download one from the URL below, or you can simply draw it out on paper. Basically, we just want to map out an information tree – drilling down into more and more detail about our individual client (and her pet).

I suggest doing one of these for as many avatars or ideal client types as you can! (it's a little different if your clients are businesses – but you can use the same idea).

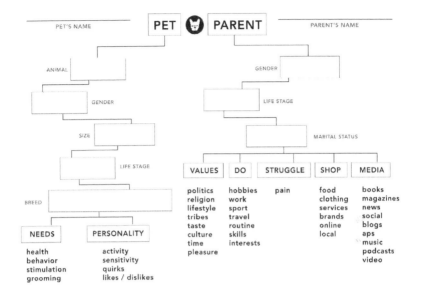

Let's Start at Pet Level:

Are you for dogs? Cats? Horses? Speak specifically to one at a time.
Since we're dog people – we're going to run with dog.
Now, get specific.

    a.   Dog's gender?

    b.   Big dog or little dog?

    c.   Purebred dog or mutt?

    d.   Old or young?

Then we drill down into the details of the dog's NEEDS and PERSONALITY:

    a.   Hairy dog or short-haired dog? (grooming needs)

    b.   Active or lazy? (exercise needs)

    c.   Laid back or nervous? (personality)

    d.   Barker? Chewer? Digger?

You want to narrow it down until you can picture the exact dog, his or her exact needs and the place it fills in its human's life. What is their routine? What does the human buy for the dog? What does having this dog mean to the human and his/her life?

These questions matter because they impact the decisions that may lead this Pet Parent to buy from you!

Next, we look to the parent:

First, we need to know if our who identified as a man or a woman. Next, we need to know what life stage he or she is at, "young" (up to 40) or "wise" (40+).
Third we need to know if this parent is in a human relationship: "single" or "couple."

Now we can drill down into some REAL detail. Let's say we're looking at Katie: a woman who is young and single. I like to assign actual names to each who so I can get to know them properly :)

The next categories to dig into or questions to answer are these:

1. What are her values?

What does she believe in, love, hate, and rally for... What is her political stance, her cultural norm, her sexual orientation, her religious belief?

Value Example:

Dog. Her dog is definitely her baby. She has mom guilt because she works all the time, but her dog walker is brilliant and he gets a good run every day. She makes a lot of decisions in life based on him – her car, her condo, even her clothes – that hair gets everywhere!

Politics. She is largely dissatisfied with current political climate and doesn't see herself represented in any of it. She generally votes Democrat because of her stance on social issues, but she's not confident in any politician she's ever seen.

Sexual Orientation. Although most people don't know this about her, she's dated both men and women. She was recently in a long-term relationship with a guy but it's people and not gender that she falls for – so she doesn't really know where she fits in to society's stereotypes.

Cultural Norms. She identifies herself as American, her mom and dad were both immigrants though so she has the benefit of being bilingual. She has a mix of cultural heritage from her parents and loving the melting-pot that is Boston, where she lives now.

2. How does she spend her time?

Where does she work, where does she take the dog, what are her skills/interests/hobbies? Where does she go on holiday?

Do Example:

Work. Demanding hours for her marketing manager gig at an agency.

Gym. At least once a week but she wishes it were more.

Shop. Usually her shopping is online, but once in a while she gets a good Saturday shopping spree in at her favorite outdoor mall.

Travel. Most of her travel is boring for work – she gets the occasional weekend away with the dog but she's been planning and saving for that trip back to Europe for the last 16 months – she hasn't been since high school.

Volunteer. Although not as often as she'd like.

Dog. She loves to take him to the lake on Sunday to watch him play and there are several trips to the dog park per week – she wishes she had more time for hiking and adventuring with him – mostly they veg out together on the couch and go for the occasional run when she gets up early enough.

3. What does she struggle with?
What gets her down? Keeps her up nights? What does she worry about or fear?

Struggle Examples:

Body image. Uh, is that MORE cellulite!? When will it stop multiplying!?

Horrible boss. Maybe it's time for her to start looking for another job.

Never-satisfied, super condescending mom. She wishes she would just back off!

Late period. Uh-oh!

Finding jeans that fit her butt. Why don't they make clothes in human sizes?

Broken heart. She wishes hhe'd call. No she doesn't. Yes, she does!

4. Where does she buy stuff?
Online, in person, for herself, for friends, for her dog – food, clothing, electronics – where does she choose to spend her hard-earned cash?

Shopping Examples:

Amazon. Who doesn't?

Zappos. Enough said.

Flash Sales. For clothes, travel, coupons – yes please I never knew I needed that!?

Designers. Kate Spade, Coach and the occasional Louboutin. They're totally for work, though, right?

Athletics. Nike, Lulu Lemon, REI.

Groceries. Whatever is closest and Whole Foods and online groceries.

Brands at the mall. Victoria's Secret, Anthropologie, Nordstrom's, Macy's, plus a sneaky bit of TJ Maxx, sash!
Electronics. Apple for phone /computer, Samsung for TV, Bose and Sonos for sound.

5. What media does she consume?

What shows does she watch on TV? What social media is she active on? Podcasts? Blogs? Magazines? Where does she get her news, gossip, advice, and entertainment?

Media Examples:

Netflix. Enough said.

Guilty-Pleasure TV. More Netflix and Real Housewives, Dancing with the Stars, American Idol.

Movies / Films. Anything with Channing Tatum, Ben Stiller, or Amy Schumer. Most of the epic series – old and new (Indiana Jones, Star Wars, Hunger Games, Lord of the Rings...) she doesn't take film super seriously she just wants to tune out and relax.

Blogs. She follows a few fashion blogs religiously. She also loves Design Sponge and Design Milk (and of course Dog Milk) but she doesn't have as much time as she used to read blogs.

News. She gets the news feed straight into her phone to browse headlines when she wakes up. Tonight Show / Saturday Night Live. She gets a lot of her current events from comedy shows. Mostly consumed on YouTube because she isn't around to watch them live.

Social:

Facebook. Pretty much all the time – definitely at work!

Twitter. Mostly when she wants to complain about something.

Instagram. When she wakes up, goes to bed, or has a free moment to browse.

Pinterest. Three to five times a month or more when she's got a project coming up she wants to get inspired for.
YouTube. She uses YouTube to create music playlists for her while she's working or to look up how-to do something and to watch comedy sketches – see above.

LinkedIn. She has a profile but pretty much only updates it if she's networking or job hunting.

Books. She likes an occasional challenge, something political or intense, but a lot of her reading is self-help or just for fun. She finally just read Big Magic, she read Harry Potter and totally loved all the Twilight and 50 Shades books (although she won't necessarily admit it because her friends would probably tease her). She loves the Jamie Oliver 15-minute meals cookbook. She always wants allll the cookbooks when she sees them.

Magazines. Marketing, Real Simple, Sunset, Dwell and the occasional sneaky gossip mag (usually on the plane or at the salon).

These questions MATTER because they impact how you are going to find and Katie and how you're going to appeal to her when you do!

Whoa. That's a lot.

The idea here is that we write her into existence. Imagine you're writing the character of a novel or screenplay – that's how well you want to know her – her back story – her motivations, struggles, and quirks. This exercise is NOT meant to eliminate everyone but Katie (although you will push some people away and that is GOOD), it's meant to get you so clear on **who Katie is** (and the two to five other avatars you create) so that you can create a habit of SPEAKING DIRECTLY TO HER when you're marketing.

In other words, knowing what you know about Katie now, it would be pretty easy to think of ideas for content, sales and promotions, and social media posts that she would like, doesn't it?

Now What?

The Ideal Client Map is for brainstorming all the items listed above. There is room at the top to add photos if you want to give your clients an actual face. I suggest creating a Word doc or similar file as well so you can write and write and write ideas, topics etc. once you've gotten started. You might find you want a whole backstory for your people once you've invested all the time in getting to know them.

If you're feeling stuck, consider these Pet Parent avatars:

- o young single female or male (no human kids)
- o young straight couple (with human kids but had the pet first)
- o young gay couple (no human kids)
- o wise single female (no human kids)
- o wise married straight couple (grown human kids)
- o wise married gay couple (no human kids)

Or these Pet Guardian avatars:

- o young single male or female (no human kids, new to pet ownership)
- o young straight couple (with human kids, got the pet for the kids)
- o wise single male or female (has some old-school beliefs about pet ownership)
- o wise married couple (no human kids, breeds and shows or works dogs)

To help with you master this "who" marketing sense, consider:

1. **Giving the dog and human names** so you can refer to them.

2. **Creating Pinterest board** for each avatar and their world.

3. **Keep their "client map" handy** so you can refer to it when working on your marketing stuff.

4. **Refer back to the sales funnel** and brainstorm content that Katie might be interested in at each stage of the funnel.

The final point I want to make about your Sense of Sight is that this is the time to start collecting data. Your first sense is all about you and your needs, desires, skills, resources etc., but from this sense onwards, the more data you can collect, the better. I just want to say that now to make sure it's clear all the way through.

You can make many of your decisions based on gut and instinct, but getting real market data, real insights from customers, and utilizing the analytics available to you is a critical part of making educated decisions.

15. Sense Three: Sense of Hearing

Ok, now you're on a roll. You know why you do what you do, and you know who you do it for. Fantastic! The third sense is all about unearthing what you do. How is your brand going to earn money?

What is It?

The third of the Marketing Senses, the Sense of Hearing, is all about listening to your who to learn what they want and are willing to pay for, so you can optimize your products and services to increase demand and profit. This sense is all about what it is that you do, sell, or offer.

Why Does it Matter?

Well, if we're all in agreement that a business exists with the sole aim of creating value (#cashmoney) than I think we can all agree that having something to sell that is actually desirable to the intended audience is pretty damn essential. I mean, if you're not interested in creating demand, profit, or influence then by all means, feel free to skip this one. But if you want to actually make a return on your investments (time, money, blood, sweat, tears) in brand-building, listen up.

Notice that the "what" is our third, and not our first step.

If you want to build a successful business and brand, it is essential to find the place where YOUR ideas, skills, resources, capabilities, and values overlap with what your WHO is actually interested in paying for.

If you don't know what your unique resources and values are, and you don't know exactly who to ask about what they want and are willing to pay for, then you are essentially gambling. You might as well just write everything you're interested in making, selling, marketing, or offering down on a big huge piece of paper, hang it on the wall, then throw darts at it. That's just about as likely to succeed as deciding on a whim that "I'm going to make collars" or "I am going to walk dogs" and just setting up shop.

Now don't get me wrong, I am all for just starting, and I am ALL for raw ambition and confidence and throwing caution to the wind, but when you look all the statistics about failing small businesses, this is why. It's not that these businesses can't sell enough stuff (although this often is an issue too of course); many of these businesses fail because they burn out.

Because they grow in too many directions too quickly with no focus, are competing based on price and lose money on each sale, or their offering might only be about 70% right, so they do well when there is little competition, but then when customers suddenly have choice, or a fancy new brand comes in to town, they go for the 100% offering, even if they have to pay more.

You with me?

What we're talking about here is getting your product strategy right for two primary reasons:

1. You
2. Them.

1. YOU:

If you are going to be the dominant force in building this brand, then EVERYTHING YOU DO WILL BE EASIER AND MORE EFFECTIVE if you love the work you're doing. If you're damn good at it, that helps a great deal, but most the important part of unearthing your "why" is so that you have (and your team has) a driving force that is bigger than you and bigger than money to push forward when the going gets tough.

2. THEM:

It doesn't matter how passionate you are about something if nobody else cares enough to buy it. Most of our great ideas are not viable Million Dollar Dog Brands because they are too complicated, too ordinary (they don't stand out), or we can't offer a competitive enough price to really build a business out of them.

If you start the MDDB process and discover during this step that actually no one is willing to pay for what you're offering, consider that a massive win. You just saved yourself months or years of brutal "forcing it"! Start again!

How Does Your "What" Show Up?

"How do you take something like a leash or a collar and make it unique? Listening and observing and addressing our customers' needs. I am continually amazed when I'm at a trade show, or I'm talking to a group of search and rescue or guide dog users and I'm talking about the features that we build into our products, and the buyer or the search and rescue handler will look at me and say, "Man, you must use your products. You get it." And I just chuckle at the fact that there are companies out there who don't even know why they're building what they are building." – Patrick, Ruffwear

Your what, is proof of your why. It's your why in action. It's the thing that allows your who to share your why with you.

It's the logical monetization of the pursuit of your why.

Example: Ruffwear

Why
I want it to be easier to share outdoor adventures with our dogs.

What
Make stuff to keep dogs safe and comfortable in challenging outdoor environments.

Remember way back in the beginning of the book, before your Why Mapping exercise when I said I wanted you to set aside who you think you are based on what you do? The same advice applies now. Time to ditch your assumptions about what you're "supposed to do" based on what you believe to be true about your job or business category.

Most petpreneurs I meet are trying very hard to be "professional," are very focused on being respected by their peers and consequentially, copy what everyone else is doing in order to fit in. Fair enough, it's generally wise to look to more experienced, successful examples in your industry to learn the ropes. But the problem is that most of THESE people did the same thing when they started. So you're copying a copy. Worse yet, you usually have no idea whether or not these people are actually successful! You might be copying someone who puts on a great show on Instagram but who is actually miserable, broke, working another job to pay the rent etc. Worse yet, when we put ourselves into existing models, boxes, or categories we lose our ability to innovate. We lose the courage to dash wildly outside the lines... and I hate to break it to you, but outside the lines is where Million Dollar Dog Brands thrive.

So what does this have to do with your "what"? Everything.
Below I will give you three different exercises to generate some ideas for how your "what" can show up, based on your "why" and "who," but I want to offer a word of warning first. When you follow the method I am suggesting here, determining your "why" first, then your "who," and THEN your "what" (rather than deciding what you do first and squeezing everything else to fit that) you may suddenly find yourself outside the lines. You might find you don't fit nicely into any existing model. You might discover that when describing your brand, or your product mix, there is no easy label to affix to it. You might find it difficult to explain "what you are." This is great news! Just answer with why you do what you do instead. You don't need to fit into a box because you're building your own!

Example:
Let's say you are a dog walker, but by working through this book you discover that you also have a strong desire and the right skill set and resources to also be a dog trainer and a pet photographer.

(By the way, this is not an uncommon grouping of skills!) What do you say you are or do when people ask you? Do you have three different websites? Do you have three different business cards? No. You take yourself out of the "dog walker" box, and out of the "dog trainer" box and out of the "pet photographer" box and you build yourself a brand: A NEW box where the services you offer totally make sense together because they all serve the pursuit of your WHY.

The trick here, is to find the thing golden string that pulls you through dog walking, training and photography. The theme, feeling, passion, or area of expertise where they all make sense. For one of my clients, that golden thread was a breed. She rebranded multiple businesses to be all under one all-Pitbull roof, offering multiple services and products just to Pitbull advocates and owners. She's now 100% aligned with all the activities where she can offer value to the group she cares most about helping!

You might discover that your why was more about being outside, or about healing from trauma, or about getting physically fit and feeling beautiful – all of which could be logically supported by dog walking, training, and photography services.

The Warning

As you can see by the example above, this work is a bit mind-bending. It's not obvious and you may find all of this un-boxing uncomfortable because the answers don't come fast enough. The unknown is dark and it may be hard to feel your way through.

You may have highs and lows, and halfway through you may question everything because it feels too messy. You may even be tempted to stop and just Google your competitor and copy what they're doing because it's so much easier to just play by everyone else's rules. Don't. Stick it out. Take a deep breath and step out into the dark; I promise you'll find light at the other side if you keep moving forward!

How to Master the "What" Sense

At its core, this third hearing sense is all about listening for opportunity. You can never have enough tools to look out into the wide world and decide what is viable and worth pursuing, and what is the preverbal "shiny object."

Below are three different ways to identify opportunities, possible whats to leverage to monetize your brand. Some of these may be handy now, some may be more handy later if you run into a spot where you're not sure how or where to grow. The next step is to filter all those possible options down into the products and services you choose to present to your customers.

1. Finding Opportunity

A) Why and Who-based Opportunity

The first exercise is a simple brainstorming and sorting exercise. I want you to get a piece of paper or two, or some digital version that suits you, and make two columns:

Column A: My Zone of Genius

Column B: What My People Want and Are Willing to Pay For

In Column A, list the items from your Why Mapping exercise and/ or products and services you know you want to offer. To jog your memory:

YOUR WHY: What do you stand for? What passion, values, and big ideas can inspire products?

YOUR SKILLS / GENIUS: What unique skills do you have that you can combine with dog training? (Language? Art? Fitness?)

YOUR RESOURCES: What unique resources do you have that give you an advantage? (Location? Experience? Relationships?)

YOUR TIME: How do you want to be spending your time? What gives you the most fulfillment?

In Column B, list all the things you know there is demand for. Based on what you uncovered in your Ideal Client Map exercise, the things you know your "who" wants and needs.

Next: Draw a simple Venn diagram: Draw two circles, one on the left, one on the right, and overlapping in the middle. On the left circle, write, "My zone of genius." On the right circle write, "What my people want and are willing to pay for." On the overlap, write what I call "The bliss point."

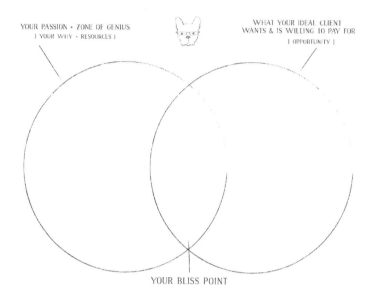

YOUR PASSION + ZONE OF GENIUS
[YOUR WHY + RESOURCES]

WHAT YOUR IDEAL CLIENT
WANTS & IS WILLING TO PAY FOR
[OPPORTUNITY]

YOUR BLISS POINT

The next step is to fill in the circles with the stuff from your columns... anything that was on both lists goes in the middle, in the bliss point. Y

our ideal "whats" are the ones which fall in the "bliss point," that intersection of your "why" and what you're "who" needs and is willing to pay for.

Wander too far to one side or the other and you're likely to be unhappy doing the work or unable to sell the product or both!

B) Pet Hierarchy of Roles-based Opportunity

The next easy way to identify opportunity is to refer back to the Pet Hierarchy of Roles Pyramid we discussed a few pages back and identify the role your ideal client is most likely to associate with: Pet Owner, Pet Guardian or Pet Parent. Next, have a look at the ideas listed for that particular role. For example, for Pet Parent the opportunities listed included:

- Force-free training tools and resources*

  * Additionally this passionate, educated consumer will expect a total absence of force or pain-causing training philosophies and tools: no pinch, no choke, no prong!

- Natural and holistic wellness
- Grain-free, single-ingredient, home cooked diets
- RAW or BARF diets
- Dietary supplements
- Organic / local products
- Enrichment toys and activities
- Premium supplies and accessories
- Design-led brands
- Premium gifts / items for Pet Parents
- Premium pet-themed or "designed with pet in mind" home goods
- Advanced problem solvers (Catios, toys for heavy chewers, advanced health services, allergies)

Is there anything in the list associated with the pet caretaker role you think your customer will fit?

2. Filtering Opportunity

Once you've identified many opportunities that would be a good fit for you and your brand, it's time to filter them. One of the most effective ways to present your products to your customers is by anchoring them in a tiered pricing model. For example, presenting a cheap version, a middle version and a premium version is an exceptionally effective way to make it easy for your client to quickly understand what you offer and which is the best fit for their needs.

The first benefit of offering this anchored model is that your customer doesn't get overwhelmed by too many choices. Too many choices leads customers to not buy, so we want to avoid that. The second benefit is that by offering a tiered model with a cheap "easy yes" product and a more premium product, the middle option becomes the most appealing. If all you offered was the middle product, it wouldn't seem quite as appealing on its own, because the cheap and premium products weren't there offering value context, whispering to your customer, "Don't take the most expensive or the cheapest, take the middle one, that's sensible." It eases guilt and makes decision-making easier.

I call these levels the "novelty," "core," and "premium" products and I recommend (for the reasons above) that you shape your strategy in this way. When you present your "what" to your "who" – offering a nice tiered set of three options (each one of course can have variations or several flavors within it) is a very effective way to encourage purchase.

This is also a helpful way to filter all the opportunities you've identified thus far into clean, easy-to-understand, easy-to-sell products or services.

Most importantly, it needs to be easy for your customer to understand from one to the next why they would want each, and which is the best fit for them. Eliminate similarity when creating these tiers and make each one distinct from the next.

Novelty Product – $

This is where you can score your first easy yes transaction:

- o Low cost
- o Low commitment
- o Low expectations
- o Can be "taster" or "trial"

Core – $$

- o This is where you'll make most of your revenue
- o Your most popular products
- o This is the product / service most people will seek you out for
- o "Cash cow"

Premium – $$$

- o If you don't have a premium offering, you're leaving money on the table
- o Your most profitable products
- o Premium products act as an anchor to make the core product seem less expensive
- o May include more access to you – more 1:1 time or increased benefits, features, or convenience

Now keep in mind, these may be individual products, or they may be individual categories of products.

Example: We learned quickly at Dog is Good that not everyone was keen or able to buy a $20 tee shirt, especially as a gift. So we created magnets, stickers and mugs with our most popular designs on them

Interestingly, sometimes people would still spend $20, but they'd feel like they got more for their money by buying 5-6 magnets or a mug and a couple stickers. We also discovered that many of our customers became repeat buyers – so if we could get them to purchase that mug for 12.99 it was very likely they'd be back for a tee or two or ten. Additionally, we learned that some of our customers were willing to spend a lot more, so we started to offer hoodies, PJ's, tote bags and other products with a higher price-point.

Dog is Good's Pricing Tiers:

Novelty (the easy yes) - $2.99-$12.99 Magnets, mugs, stickers, cards

Core (most of what we sold) - $19.99-$29.99 Tees, Hats

Premium (higher end products) - $39.99-$49.99 – Hoodies, PJ's

This worked very well for us to be able to promote the tees for less, or create bundles of multiple good for more. Equally, it allowed virtually anyone who loved our brand to buy something and become a part of our community.

Summing it Up

Obviously, pricing and product strategy is a very complex topic and the suggestions above are simply a guideline to make your offering simple, desirable and anchored in value to make decision-making easy for your customer.

Crafting the right 'what' for your 'who' to serve as proof of your 'why' is the constant work of a business. These dynamic people and ideas will change, and evolve all the time, but if you start with offering stuff you know your who wants and are willing to pay for, and presenting it in the tiered pricing model, you should be well on your way to keeping that sales funnel full and productive!

16. Sense Four: Sense of Touch

"I have a pretty strong vision when it comes to the look and feel of the brand. It's definitely evolved several times over the years. We've kind of updated and evolved the look and feel of our packaging and website. It's gone from I think what was probably a bit more of a clinical kind of metal feel, to something that feels a lot more foodie and culinary. We work with an amazing artist called Natalya Zahn who's based in Massachusetts to create paintings that are on our packaging and a lot of the art that's on our website as well. So, everything feels very cohesive." – Lucy, Honest Kitchen

So, now you know why you do what you do, who you do it for, and what you sell. The next step is to determine the way your brand shows up aesthetically: on your website, your trade show booth, in your ads and everywhere else where your who will experience you.

What is It

The fourth of the Marketing Senses, the Sense of Touch, is all about optimizing the places where your who will experience your brand. In marketing lingo, we call these places (your website, business card, event booth, social media etc.) "touch points." This sense is your "where."

This is the moment when we start to focus on the aesthetic parts of your brand. What this means is that from this moment forward, your responsibility is to care deeply about things you might not have ever noticed before. If you're going to be the owner of a brand, your job is to be its number one defender. This means being ruthlessly discerning and consistent, sometimes even obsessive about things like fonts, logo usage, color, and general design whenever your brand is involved.

Why Does it Matter?

This sense is the one I think most people automatically associate with the word "brand." This sense is where your logo, packaging, website, and printed materials start to develop. This sense is all about the artefacts of your brand that your clients can actually see, touch, and hear. This stuff matters not just because it's pretty, but because this is how all the other senses will be delivered. This sense is the vehicle to communicate your why. This is the sense that dictates what kind of emotional response your audience will have, which as we agreed earlier, is the whole goal of any marketing you do. Right?

How Does it Show Up?

Our brains processes visual information 60,000 times faster than text, so like it or not, the aesthetics of your brand have a much faster and more profound ability to hit your customer right in the feels. But when you set about creating anything for your business (a postcard, a newsletter, a catalog, or an email) it's easy to feel like you're starting over each time. Like you have to reinvent that emotional impact differently on everything!

Building a brand helps you get away from that constant reinvention by allowing you to create winning formulas and shortcuts to achieve consistent results. For example, you can use the same tagline, the same photos in the same layout over and over again.

Many businesses have brand guidelines or a style guide which are both very valuable tools to help with this consistency (I will talk about brand guidelines later). But for now, I want to share with you the 10 most important elements you'll use when designing some of these formulas for your brand. I call this collection of elements your Marketing Toy Box.

I could literally write an entire book on each and every one of these 10 toys, so in the interest of making this as simple and easy to implement as possible, I am just going give you some simple tips for each. Of course, in Working with Dog we provide tons of help and resources for this stuff (our members are constantly posting their marketing touchpoints in the group to get our advice) so if you're rebranding or building a new brand, definitely consider making use of our community!

How to Master the "Where" Sense

Below you'll see a list of 10 essential toys in your Marketing Toy Box. I call this kit the toy box because I want you to remember to be playful with your customers.

To keep it light, to appeal to their senses. To take risks. To dive for the ball. To be more human, or more dog... be cute, be funny, be sophisticated... be anything except robotic!

This list is in order of importance, which is determined by:

1. **Efficacy:** How effective the toy is at making an instant emotional connection with your potential client.

2. **Frequency:** How easy the toy is to implement and how often you have the chance to use it.

For example, some toys, like video for example, are extremely effective but not always possible to use (easy digitally but impossible in print) - so it gets pushed a bit lower down the list. The top five: images, color, social proof, graphics, and space are the toys you can use most often (in person, in print, and online) and with the greatest impact on creating curiosity, desire, or to stir other feelings within your potential customer.

Marketing Toy Box

1. Imagery
2. Color
3. Social Proof
4. Graphics
5. Space
6. Copy
7. Audio / Video
8. Touch / Texture
9. Smell / Taste
10. X-Factor

In the following pages I will give you five quick tips for each of these plus some examples from our MDDBs and a few other inspiring brands.

1. Imagery

"In terms of branding and marketing, one of the very important things we did early on was to invest in photography. If you want to convey a lifestyle, consumers aren't going to have the benefit of hearing your story in first-person narrative... they will see your website, maybe a flyer. In the case of business-to-business buyers, they rely on looking at your packaging or your collateral at trade shows. I think the fundamental building block to that is getting your story right – but next after that is photography. Product photography, but especially lifestyle images. Pet products are especially emotional purchases. I think seeing a good lifestyle photo of a dog enjoying a most comfortable nap is better than reading a whole page of selling points, saying why our beds are better."
– Will, P.L.A.Y.

"Since the beginning, we realized how important imagery is and how important the quality of the imagery is for a better perception of product quality. I'm not sure how clear that sounds, but if you look at a product, and the picture's really bad, even though the product's really good, your brain is telling you that maybe it's not as good. We wanted to make sure that with the pictures we really showcased what we're about. I can say the product is for a particular lifestyle, but if people don't see it then it's hard for them to really believe it. If they don't believe it then they don't want to be part of it. So it's a critical part of the authenticity of the brand. Being able to actually replicate, in an authentic way, our own lifestyle helps keep our brand desirable.

Also, we're very aesthetically demanding. I'm very, very anal about quality of pictures and imagery and graphics. We have a huge design team internally. We do everything ourselves, we don't use agencies. I've always been a firm believer that I need to have them on board, in house and have that DNA running through our blood, to really be able to replicate this on an ongoing scale.

The images from Instagram to Facebook, the videos that we've done... the people in them, in truth it's really me and three other kids. But we are very, very, very careful with the imagery that we put out. Just to top that off, we have brought back film. We do a lot of our pictures in 35mm. I don't do a lot of digital; I do more digital when it comes to product shots and studio stuff, but you'll see that most of our pictures are analog. People will say, 'Wow, it's such a modern company, but you're bringing back a lot of old-school things.' The main reasons why I do that is that one, I think film photography will always look better than digital, and two, I think it's a bit reminiscent for people our age; we were able to still have a bit of that era of analog photography in our childhood. Anything that's reminiscent has an emotional connection. As you know, emotion makes people buy." – Thad, Zee.Dog

"To communicate to customers, dealers, or retailers what we're all about, who we are, we just present pictures of what we're doing with our dogs in the environment that we intend the gear to perform in. None of this was obvious to me when we started, it was just a bumbling along, learning-as-I-go process. When it came to shooting our images, we just wanted to take photos of our products in the element that they were designed for. The turning point for us was when we started making dog boots; I noticed a big shift in our photography. Rather than taking a picture of a dog drinking out of a bowl or a dog wearing a backpack, we had to get down at the dog level. We had to be almost underneath the dog to get that image of their footwear. If you notice, most of our photography is from the dog's perspective and I think that is a really telling part of a shift in Ruffwear, that we always knew but hadn't said. We don't design from the human down, we design from the dog up. Our products are based on dog-centric needs, so, our photography is really about the dog's perspective." – Patrick, Ruffwear

So, let's just start by being clear that I am a commercial photographer. It is only in the last year or so that I have set my camera down to focus entirely on marketing, so admittedly, there is bias inherent in this bit, but I also have over 12 years of real-world experience purchasing, utilizing, and watching the impact of powerful imagery in action. What I can tell you is that when you have one or two seconds to capture a distracted consumer (which is everywhere these days) unless you are competing based on price,

there is no sales tool MORE effective per dollar spent than aspirational, emotive lifestyle imagery (still and video).

Interestingly, despite the precedent set by larger brands who spend heavily on lifestyle imagery, nearly all entrepreneurs I meet invest virtually nothing in the creation of images that tell their brand story.

Most companies dabble in photography... what I mean is, most businesses know they need product photos or stock photos to fill up their website, but it is quite rare to meet a small business owner who really, really "gets it" when it comes to photography. It's like the best kept non-secret in marketing! I am not suggesting you spend on photography for the fun of it; remember this book is about creating profit, not just something pretty. Both my real-life experience and post-graduate academic study support the fact that brands who use lifestyle imagery in their marketing and sales efforts profit immensely.

"The lifestyle product shots that were taken have helped fuel our 2000% sales growth and will continue to be a main driver in our sales as we grow online." - Sarah, Denhaus

Part of the reason lifestyle images are so effective is because they show context (where and how the product could be used for maximum enjoyment).

Part of the reason they work is because they infuse emotion into a service or a thing: showing them being used by humans or pets (or humans and pets together) makes them relatable to us and our own lives.

Part of the magic is that when done well, these images activate the visceral response we humans have to pleasing visual aesthetics. Donald Norman, author of Emotional Design sums this process up beautifully,

"Because visceral design is about initial reactions, it can be studied quite simply by putting people in front of a design and waiting for reactions. In the best of circumstances, the visceral reaction to appearance works so well that people take one look and say, "I want it." Then they might ask, "What does it do?" And last, "And how much does it cost?" This is the reaction the visceral designer strives for, and it can work." — Donald A. Norman, Emotional Design: Why We Love (or Hate) Everyday Things

We like pretty things. They make our brain happy. Especially the part of our brain responsible for purchase-based decision making.

As I mentioned before, I could write a whole book on each one of these marketing toys so I'll cut this short by simply saying this:

If you do not have lifestyle imagery for your brand (professional photos of you, the product or service in action in beautiful scenes / settings and with aesthetically pleasing animals and humans) then promise me you will make that a priority in the next six months.

Just so you know, "professional" does not have to cost the earth. Depending on who you use, or how many products you have, $500-$1000 is plenty to get you a few outstanding shots that you can plaster everywhere.

If you can comfortably budget more like $2k-$5k you can work with some of the best pet photographers in the industry. Want to know who? You can email my team at hello@workingwithdog.com and we are happy to match-make for you based on your brand, product or location. Otherwise, just Google "pet photography 'yourcity'. Look for a page called "commercial photography" or "for small businesses" on the photographers' website.

HINT: If you're a service provider and you're looking mostly to get some good action shots of you at work plus some detail shots of your brand swag or tools of the trade, it's definitely worth considering wedding photographers. In most cases they are used to giving away high-res images and are usually comfortable working in multiple locations and tricky lighting environments. Look for one with pets in their portfolio!

5 Quick and Useful Imagery Tips:

1. When selecting imagery of dogs / cats / people on their own – it is FAR more engaging to have them looking straight at you (the viewer) than with their head turned. Publishers know this is the first trick to getting dog books / magazines picked up off the shelf. If you're selling a product, the pet looking at or interacting with the product is also quite effective.

2. For maximum emotional impact and desire-building, be sure to include detail imagery in your marketing. I describe these as the "yummy filler shots" – images with sharp focus and shallow depth of field (blurry background) where there is more lifestyle or result implied than actual technical aspects of a product or service perfectly depicted. Think of these as the "moments" in the life of your ideal people. For example: worn leather leash and keys on the counter to sell dog walking... dog sleeping on the couch with beautiful portrait of him on wall above to sell pet photography... happy dog sitting look up at you to sell dog treats. Behind-the-scenes textures that can trigger sense experiences will do the trick (especially in the days when all of our websites have places for huge images with text over them). Example: treats = chopped fresh ingredients on a cutting board; collars = piles of materials or hand-cutting, hand sewing close-ups.

3. Because our brains process visual information 60,000 times FASTER than text – show it rather than say it, whenever possible. Resist the urge to over explain and just let an image do the selling. Better yet – let a VIDEO or CINEMAGRAPH do the selling – imagery doesn't have to be static! (See #6 audio/video.)

4. Stock images that look like stock lose nearly all of the emotional impact because they feel fake and unrealistic. This doesn't mean you can't use stock imagery (although I'd always say it pays to get your own library of images). It just means you need to choose images that look natural and that make you feel something when you look at them. I love CreativeMarket.com for not-your-average images – or you can go to the usual suspects (Shutterstock, Getty) and just be very selective about the images you choose. For better-than-average free stock, check out unsplash.com.

5. Investing in great photography is one of the best things you can do for your brand, but if you're personal brand or a serviced based business, invest in a library of great images of you: headshots alone, lifestyle images of you with your pets, day-to-day running of your business, and detail shots of what you do will be INCREDIBLY VALUABLE. You'll need these not only to build credibility and trust, but also to send along for PR, guest speaking / blogging / appearances and press that might come your way, in addition to, of course, telling your story digitally (on a website, Facebook, Instagram etc.) in a compelling way.

In Action:

Zee.Dog us.zee-dog.com | @zeedog
You read what Thad said about how important imagery is to zee dog. Go check out how inspiring, beautiful, colorful, edgy, playful, and warm the Zee.Dog images are! Their own photography is consistent and the work they curate (user generated) fits in so well, it's often hard to tell the difference between "ours" and "theirs." Who wants to buy a new collar or leash now?

2. Color

One of the quickest ways creatures make decisions about things is through the interpretation of color. Not just humans, either: Think of all those crazy-colored birds, bugs, and reptiles that use color as a way to scare off predators, attract mates, or send other messages about where they fit in to the circle of life. We all know color is an incredibly important element in our decision-making, especially when it comes to what we buy, but check it:

"Customers generally make an initial judgment on a product within 90 seconds of interaction with that product and about 62%-90% of that judgment is based on color."[8]

Your customers and clients are operating under this same code of conduct, so color becomes an essential element in your ability to attract and communicate with them before they have a chance to meet you or read a single thing you have to say. Make sure the colors you are using are consistent to your brand and are a good fit for the product you're selling and your price / position in the market. You want to ensure the colors you're using are giving your clients all the right feels. If you're selling a product that will end up in their home, you better make sure that product matches their couch, curtains, wallpaper, etc.!

Want Help?

Want your own brand color palette selected and designed by me and my team? Visit workingwithdog.com/color and send us an image or two you'd like us to use for your custom palette.

For examples, check out #dogcolorpalette on Instagram. Pinterest is another great place to explore color. Simply search for "color palette" or a specific color and you will be treated with ALL KINDS of inspiration. You can also use our 'Color Dog' board on Pinterest at pinterest.com/withdog/.

---

[8] https://en.wikipedia.org/wiki/Color_psychology

5 Quick and Useful Color Tips:

1. Your eye is automatically drawn to the lightest (whitest) thing on a page. This is essential when you're creating an ad or marketing piece with an important call-to-action or headline you want to be the most obvious message on the page – make it the lightest thing. When in doubt, add darker background for bright/light call-out.

2. Primary colors (fire engine red, grass green, royal blue, bright yellow) have a tendency to look childish or basic – do not use these together in designs you're hoping will look elegant or premium. White, black ,and grey are often the signature colors of "premium" or "elegance" and carefully selected "pop" colors can add interest and excitement. But beware, monochromatic or one-color designs can easily be boring and uninspiring, so you'll need colorful imagery if the brand/website is monochrome.

3. If you have a white background, try using medium to dark grey text instead of black to soften the harshness of the black on white. For text, more often than not, use dark on light – light text on a dark background is usually harder (and more tiring) to read.

4. For products that will end up in your clients' home – note that earth tones (brown, green, blue, and greys) are the most common choices because they match the majority of wood and carpet combos that most people have. That's not to say you can't go BOLD in color – but keep in mind when you produce that hot pink dog bed that it has to match a room in someone's home (ideally the living room) or they won't buy it. For products that will have a dog on, in, or anywhere near it – most Pet Owners know that dog is going to be muddy and hairy so often they will opt for a darker color to avoid doing more clean up than is necessary. If you make a product that will be sold off a shelf, go look at the shelves in the stores where your product will sit!

Have a look at the colors currently displayed there and brainstorm ways that you can ensure your product stands out to the person passing by, but also compels them to choose your product because it's a good fit (i.e. don't use a color just for shock value – but be sure you're not blending into a sea of sameness).

HINT: Color is quite cultural. The advice above is for an American or Western European market, but check out what Will has to say about color in other markets:

"Every country has a difference in aesthetic preference. In Asia, there tends to be a bigger segment of people who are looking for cute things, so that's where some of our plush toys do very well, because they look cute. Actually, it's the exact opposite in Europe; we just had a potential distributor say, "I love your wobble ball but I think it's too cutesy." So, you can't please everyone. You need to either develop more products and have something for different people, or you focus on one direction and just know that you can't be everything to everyone. And there's no right or wrong in this. You know, the other day I was also listening to a company that sells a lot to Latin America, and they told me that Latin American people just love colors. I have not been myself, but I can imagine. Places like Brazil and Argentina, people love bright colors – red, yellow, orange, green. Whereas from experience, we know that selling in America as well as mostly in Europe, you need to have earth tones, you need to have darker colors, because people just find that more suitable for their household. So, as you go international it's important. Some products have no issue of such at all; let's say if you're selling shampoo, or a comb for a pet, it doesn't really quite matter, as long as you have a product with really superior function – maybe packaging, you'd have to think about packaging, but for products like beds and toys, these are very tactile and very visual products, it's important for us to look at trends and preferences and things like that." - Will, P.L.A.Y.

In Action:

Found My Animal foundmyanimal.com | @foundmyanimal
Found My Animal has used color as the primary sales tool to
differentiate one product to the next (as well as seasons of product)
but they have also managed to incorporate their "adopt don't shop"
mission directly into their product with color. Their dayglow orange
collar and lead set is affectionately called "orange rescue collar" and
the first line of the product description is "Orange is the color of
animal protection awareness..."

2 Hounds Design www.2houndsdesign.com | @2_hounds_design
After getting a better understanding how their customers shop, we
added a "shop by color" element to the 2 Hounds website navigation
(allowing pink addicts to shop only pink, or make it easier to find a
matching collar or leash). Not a bad idea if you have a lot of
colorways for the products you sell!

3. Social Proof

"We do an annual benchmarking survey to track the positive
health improvements that people see in their pets when they feed
the food, so that's been really instrumental in terms of social proof
and word of mouth. This allows a lot of our customers to kind of do
the marketing for us in many cases." – Lucy, Honest Kitchen

"In our most recent wholesale catalogue, we actually have a
testimonial of somebody who's had the same products from us for
over ten years. And she actually sent them to us, we took pictures of
them, and she said we had to send them back because her German
Shepherds, even though they aren't the same German Shepherds,
still use the same toys." – Stephanie, Planet Dog

In the age of Amazon, it's likely you already know first-hand the power of social proof – the review – the testimonial – the "as seen in." This is one of your greatest not-so-secret weapons in the battle for attention and conversions. Many of us really don't bother with making this one a priority because we don't like asking for praise. It feels like a lot of work to acquire, edit, and post testimonials, and generally feel like the whole thing is a bit "rah rah go me" – but now is the time to let those beliefs go. You HAVE GOT to be using this marketing booster in your branding. Like, right now. Also, if you are using it but it's buried on some inner client praise page that no one sees, go today and spread those testimonials throughout your site (especially on the home page, front and center).

Here's why:

"72% say reading a positive customer review increases their trust in a business; it takes, on average, 2-6 reviews to get 56% of them to this point."[9]

"Online consumer reviews are the second-most trusted form of advertising with 70 percent of global consumers surveyed online indicating they trust this platform, an increase of 15 percent in four years."[10]

"To get the most out of social proof, incorporate elements of it into your homepage design where your visitor's attention is at its highest."[11]

---

[9] https://www.brightlocal.com/learn/local-consumer-review-survey-2014/]

[10] http://www.nielsen.com/us/en/press-room/2012/nielsen-global-consumers-trust-in-earned-advertising-grows.html

[11] https://blog.hubspot.com/marketing/conversion-lessons-critiquing-100-websites#sm.00000kn4bp3u1fd77uhc19r30kbcj

Here are a few examples of social proof to consider adding or using:

- o "As seen in" logos
- o Reviews / testimonials
- o Before and after images
- o Stars (Feefo, Trust Pilot, Yelp, Facebook or similar star-rating)
- o Awards
- o Certifications
- o Partnerships
- o Influencer platforms (social feeds)

5 Quick and Useful Social Proof Tips:

1. When you go about gathering feedback, instead of just asking for a testimonial, send a short list of questions (or an actual survey) to clients and help lead them into feedback that is helpful for you. You can then edit that into shorter, more concise testimonials. As an added part of this process, make a habit of collecting an image to go along with your testimonials or reviews. When posted together, the review and photo combo significantly enhances the efficacy of the social proof.

2. If you want to increase public reviews for your business, you can use a free Google+ page, a listing on Yelp.com, and if you classify yourself as a local business you can enable reviews on Facebook. The best bet, however, is to get an account with Trust Pilot or Feefo. If you're serious about using social proof in your sales process, these are very trusted resources to help you build a reliable third-party rating.

3. Another very popular and effective way to show social proof is via the ol' "As Seen In" or "Press" page. Having "award winning" is the same. You'll notice I have this right at the top of workingwithdog.com. This is a way for us to build credibility based on the celebrity associated with the different press outlets that have interviewed us or featured our work / products. If you have them, it is well-worth gathering the press features and logos of notable press to use in this way.

4. Stars graphics are a shockingly effective tool for increasing click-through rate to your site. To get some lovely stars to use in your business, work on getting rated by a local publication that offers star-rating to local businesses, get those reviews enabled on Facebook as mentioned above, or best of all, work on getting those stars to appear near your website in Google search results. To do that, you need to enable that Google+ page for your business or join a third-party review site like Feefo or Trust Pilot and get at least 30 reviews. This strategy takes time and you'll need to consistently communicate with your clients about where they can leave the reviews for you, but eventually those stars will pop up in Google. No matter where your stars come from, consider creating a start graphic and including it on your business card, website, sales materials etc. - we are programmed to assume that four or five stars means quality and happy customers!

5. One of the most compelling forms of social proof is the before and after image. We've all seen this technique with weight-loss sales materials – it's just so hard to deny the power of a photo that shows significant transformation. Combine that with personal words about the journey from one photo another and boom. Sold. Is there a way you can use this powerful tool to show the transformation that occurs for clients in your business?

In Action:

The Blissful Dog www.theblissfuldog.com | @theblissfuldog
This example comes straight from one of our Working with Dog
members. The Blissful Dog sells that glorious "nose butter" and
other balms for your dog's dry, cracked skin. Our Frenchie has
always had a cracked nose, and every time I look at it I want to fix
it for him. When I scroll down the Blissful Dog home page, I see
tons of before and after shots – Frenchie and Bullie noses much like
Charlie's. Alongside are compelling testimonials, all of which makes
me feel confident that if I order this product, I will get the results I
am looking for.

4. Graphics

When we get to a website, we don't want to have to think. We don't
read. It's time consuming. It's an investment. We skim. We make a
judgment within a few seconds as to whether or not to make that
investment in you or your business. As I mentioned with imagery,
you're always better off showing rather than telling.

The use of graphics and illustrations can offer similar benefits as
photography to connect emotionally with your audience, but they
can also make reading faster and more efficient (think descriptive
icons). Anything that makes life easier for your potential customer
is a winning tool!

5 Quick and Useful Graphics Tips:

1. Collect a library or style of graphics that you use throughout your
marketing – either different versions of your own brand character
if you have one (your logo critter in different scenarios)
or a collection of icons with similar style: modern, vintage,
cartoony, watercolor, hand-drawn, etc.

The more unique these graphics are to your brand, the more effective they are at creating a memorable connection with your peeps. Consider commissioning custom illustrations to push your brand that bit further – this is especially effective if you're communicating a great deal with your clients (via newsletter, magazine etc.) or if you can translate those drawings into sellable products or engaging images to create engagement in social media.

2. Don't forget the king of graphics, the INFOGRAPHIC. This is a fantastic, social-media-friendly way to encourage the understanding and sharing of information relating to what it is that you're all about. We have curated a few great examples on our Info Dog board on Pinterest at pinterest.com/withdog/infodog/.

3. If you have complicated information to explain (instruction manual, complicated manufacturing process or a product or service that solves a complex problem), consider investing in a series of illustrations to explain it, rather than writing 10 pages no one will read. You can even have the illustrations animated into a video quite easily and affordably.
This is 1000x more effective than using text (that is a made-up statistic, but trust me, your customers will thank you!)

4. Your most important graphic is your logo. The most repeated visual cue you'll use to say, "Hi, this is me." Your logo is important but not so important that you need to spend a fortune right away (just think of Twitter, when they started they used a clip-art bird!) If you're on a tight budget just keep your logo simple and invest in your brand in other ways for now, like lifestyle photography. Need a quick and easy logo on the cheap? Check out 99designs.com.
This is a great resource to just get something simple done so you can move forward. Later, you can find the perfect designer for you and then you can enjoy investing in the process of gorgeous, custom brand identity package.

5. Ready to hire someone seriously AWESOME for your branding / illustration? A personal referral is always a good start. If you know someone who has branding you just can't get enough of, ask them who designed it! Keep in mind that you want to pick someone based on the work they do well – you want that work to match up with what you think you have in your head. Things may go badly if you want someone who specializes in crisp, type-heavy logos to do a cartoony caricature for you.

In Action:

BarkBox (Bark and Co.) www.barkbox.com | @barkbox
Check out the custom illustrations Bark & Co. uses throughout their branding and sub-branding – these arty, quirky, accessible, often funny little drawings give cohesion to bring all the sub-brands together, and make you smile even on their customer service pages or in their email pop-up.

P.L.A.Y. www.petplay.com @petplaysf
I love the way P.L.A.Y uses both icons and custom illustrations in their products, sales materials and all over their website. Check out the home page and the About Us page - they use easy-to-skim graphics to help you shop or get where you want to go quickly and easily.

Honest Kitchen www.thehonestkitchen.com | @honestkitchen
Go check out the custom illustrations HK commissioned for their website and packaging. Can you see how much warmth and approachability they add to a digital space or a product on the shelf? Instant like and trust!

Need Help?

We have just launched an exclusive creative agency service for building one-of-a-kind pet brands.

If you're in the market for a top-of-the-line identity package or brand refresh for your Million Dollar Dog Brand, have a look at workingwithdog.com/build-your-pet-brand/.

5. Space

One of the most common mistakes I see in small business marketing is not letting the message "breathe." Any available space gets filled with text, images, deals, descriptions, numbers, etc. Not only does this reek of desperation and insecurity – "I don't know what they want so I'll throw it all in there" – but it usually ruins the effectiveness of most forms of marketing or advertising.

When I was doing a lot of graphic design work, my clients often used this one word to describe what they wanted, or what they liked about my style... this word sums up what I want for your designs and marketing assets too. That word is: clean.

I often compare the marketing assets you're creating (like your website) to your home: You're inviting your customers in; you need to make them feel welcome and anticipate their needs so the experience is easy, pleasant, and encourages a repeat visit. So, step number one when you know someone is coming over to your house is to CLEAN IT! De-clutter. Tidy up.

Make ROOM for the wonderful experience that will unfold in your space. The same goes for your postcards, ads, business cards, etc. Leave room for your customer to take it in. Leave space for them to move around visually or physically – to feel expansive and stress free. Not convinced? Think of the difference between shopping at a luxurious boutique or department store, versus a TJ MAXX style discount shop. What's the primary difference? SPACE – room to move and browse, more space on the racks with fewer hangers crammed in, and bigger dressing rooms.

Another element of space is organization. Making it clear where your customer is, and where they need to go next.

Breaking down user guides or welcome packets or even your website navigation into an obvious start-to-finish flow that is intuitive to follow, again allows them to feel happy, relaxed, and open to the possibilities.

5 Quick and Useful Space and Layout Tips:

1. Much like your possessions, when in doubt, remove. Less is always, always, always more. What words, images, graphics, concepts etc. can you cut out and keep (or improve) the meaning or sentiment while inviting more white space into the design? This white space is not a waste, it's an investment. Consider that beautiful, white, spacious Apple packaging...

2. Bigger images are usually better. You know those great magazines (I love Sunset) where you see a full spread of some beautiful canyon and then somewhere there's a little headline and like five little lines of text and that's it? Yeah, do that. This presentation is so much more powerful than the opposite composition (tons of text and tiny image). Go big with your images both online and in print. Look around. You'll find more and more websites, blogs, full-page ads and billboards of big successful brands featuring huge imagery and a tiny bit of text. Not because they don't have much to say, or many products to sell, but because they know what works!

3. Get a pro involved. If this is not your strength (and you already know the answer to this) then delegate! I cannot over-emphasize the value of having professional layouts for your essential business tools. Luckily, this does not have to be expensive! You can quickly find great, affordable designers on Upwork.com if you have a catalog, eBook or custom project you need done.

You can also purchase gorgeous, done-for-you templates from companies like Design Aglow and Creative Market, or wonderful, responsive WordPress themes from Theme Forest. With tons of options for less than $50, there is no excuse to have a cluttered catalog or a sub-par sales kit.

4. Sort out your physical space. The space you spend your time in has a huge impact on how productive and happy you are. If you're struggling to concentrate, clean something. File those files, get rid of the extra piles of stuff in the corner. A clean and tidy office or desk, is a blank canvas for you to paint your magic on. A clutter-free room helps create a clutter-free mind and a ticked-off to-do list!

5. Struggling to fit it all in? Focus. Are you trying to be everything to everyone? Stop it. Just push out one concept, one emotion, one message, one call to action at a time (not 100 products, ideas, packages, or promotions). This is the confidence piece. Don't try to sell four things in a three-inch by four-inch space. Sell your why, or sell one thing and make it intriguing enough to get whoever is viewing it back over to your website.

In Action:

Victoria Stilwell Dog Training Academy   www.vsdta.com
When creating this site we used very purposeful blocks to indicate sections. There is an abundance of airy space surrounding text, and a purposeful alternating of content (text then image then text) to break up any large areas of any one type of content. Notice how this makes the site feel more bite-sized to read and explore – nothing is daunting or overwhelming.

The Sage Hound   thesagehound.com | @thesagehound
This Million Dollar Dog Brand that we helped build last year
belongs to one of our Working with Dog members. What I love
about this site is the incredible ease I feel moving through it.
Everything is clear, neatly organized, succinct and uncluttered. This
is a great example of all the Marketing Toys, but I think the
spaciousness, clear navigation, and large images are especially
impactful.

6. Copy

Because we are a species of talkers, and copy is often the easiest
thing to produce, we often rely more heavily on it in our marketing
than we should. As previously discussed, in our chaotic, fast-paced
world, it is almost always faster and more compelling to deliver
your message with images, color, or graphics... but a few finely
crafted words can be just the thing to tip someone over the edge of
casual observer to avid fan. Just remember, language is a fine art
and in the case of text – more is not better!

When in doubt, revisit the Brand Voice section of this book to
remind you what your goals are. More on personality, less on
"professionalism."

5 Quick and Useful Copy Tips:

1. One of the most simple ways to make large amounts of copy
more easy to skim is by breaking it into logical chunks (putting
more paragraph breaks in) and adding bullet points or lists to
highlight points. This has a positive effect on your composition
visually, making it appear less daunting to consume.

2. When you are working on copy, one of the best ways to edit is to read it out loud. Anywhere you stumble, find yourself tripping over words or not getting crystal-clear meaning... edit. Delete. Move words. Remove adjectives. Shorten the number of syllables. Make the ideas flow in a way that is easy to understand and easy to say.

3. If you struggle with copy, consider hiring a copywriter. A bit like design, copywriting is a finely crafted skill, and if you struggle to make your headlines or packaging copy exciting, hire someone who can! This skill is another one that is often underutilized and under appreciated by entrepreneurs. (For the first several years of my business I had never even heard of a copywriter!) But the copy (words, text, headlines etc.) that you use to pitch your business, sell your product, explain your offerings, etc. is another very critical extension of your brand. Crafting the voice of your business may be something that comes naturally to you, but if it doesn't, call in the pros, especially on your packaging and sales pages!

4. The most important tip when it comes to copy and text is to trim, trim, trim. There is always more to cut. It is simplicity and editing that make copy its very strongest, not quantity or complexity of words. Chop, chop, chop. Do not get attached to your beautiful words - only care for the meaning you want your client to glean from reading, and know that if there is too much or it doesn't grab them right away, they won't read it at all! On your website you can always add a "read more" option for those who want the full and complete story, but as a default, don't feel you need to explain every nuance or every detail. Just deliver the core meaning or message. Always remember that the core message should be about addressing the needs/wants of your customer or client, not stroking your own ego!

5. An important visual element of copy is font choice. I like for a brand to have at least four to five fonts in its brand guidelines: one for copy, one for headlines, one for sub-headers and one fun font. When creating large blocks of copy like this book, a serif font (like this one) is traditionally the most pleasing and familiar to the human eye. Also, when you're constrained by the options online, you sometimes don't have a lot of choice, so having a font in your pack that is easily replaced with an old stand-by like Times is helpful to keep consistency across channels. When creating eye-catching headlines, a more simple, thicker, or bolder font is often ideal (think of a poster or book cover to be seen from a distance). I often like to have a thinner, cleaner or an all-caps font for sub-headings (to compliment both the copy and header fonts). Last but not least, it's nice to have a lovely little accent font – a script, a typewriter font, a handwritten font – something very connected to who you are as a company and the emotions you want to embody as a brand.

In Action:

The Honest Kitchen | www.thehonestkitchen.com/
Check out the brand voice of Honest Kitchen. With a word like "honest" in your name, you have to bring it with the fresh, real copy and they do just that:

"Honest to goodness foods. Humans aren't the only ones who enjoy a quality meal. Set the mystery pellets aside, and let your pup or kitty dip a paw into a taste test of healthy, wholesome, proper food for pets."

7. Audio / Video

"I sat down with my team and asked, "How can we get the message out about puppy mills? Don't get a puppy from a pet store, say no to puppy mills." We had just helped with a big puppy mill bust here where I live in Georgia, where we rescued 357 dogs and puppies. There was this one puppy that wasn't meant to live, but somehow he made it. But he was so tiny, he was paired with a kitten in a shelter, and they became best friends. So we just went to go film them. We put it up on YouTube with 'the cutest puppy and kitten best friends' as the tagline. It started slow, and then all of a sudden the numbers started to go up. Sometimes 10,000 a day. Now it's at 5,992,589 views (at the time of writing the book the video now has 8.5 million views) and it's literally a one-and-a-half-minute video of this puppy and this kitten playing, with some music in the background, nicely edited together. But at the end it has the message: 'This puppy was rescued from a puppy mill. Fortunately, he survived, he was very sick but he survived and he's now in a great home.' (And we put a picture of him as an adult.) 'But there's still many more like him who need help - adoption saves lives, say no to puppy mills.' So we got our message out, but we gave them a cute little video to watch in return." – Victoria Stilwell **

** Watch the video Victoria Stilwell mentions and get additional video tips from her in episode 1 of our podcast: workingwithdog.com/podcast/s1/e1-victoria_stilwell/.

The more immersive the experience you create, the easier it is to connect with your client. Music and video can transport your message instantly past the gatekeepers of our attention – the defenses we keep at the ready to protect us from the noise of being sold-to. Both audio and video (or both) tell us what we need to know more quickly than reading, and also have the ability to entertain or connect better than just about any other medium. We are all getting the message that we need to incorporate more multimedia into our marketing and branding, but this can be daunting if it's new to us. A video added to the home page of your website could quickly become your #1 sales tool, so don't let your fear hold you back. Need some more convincing? How about these stats?

"4X as many consumers would prefer to watch a video about a product than to read about it."[12]

 "Video appears in 70% of the top 100 search results, while websites that incorporate it tend to see two more minutes of on-screen time than those that don't."[13]

You cannot wait any longer to get comfortable with video and start integrating it into your marketing.

[12] https://animoto.com/blog/business/video-marketing-cheat-sheet-infographic/

[13] https://www.crayon.co/success/state-of-video-report/

5 Quick and Useful Audio / Video Tips:

1. To move past fear, challenge yourself to just record a few casual videos with your phone or laptop, upload them to Facebook or YouTube, and share them with your existing audience. Just try it. An excellent option here is to consider a video blog, or video how-to's to supplement your blog as a way of teaching and getting clients familiar with your work. This is a must-do if you're a dog trainer!

2. Music is a great tool to help set a happy tone to your video or audio (podcast). Have a look at a site like audiojungle.net and find a couple tracks that make you feel good or give you the right energy when you listen to the first 10-20 seconds. This is royalty-free music you can purchase and use over and over in your future audio/video spots.

3. You don't even have to have or create video footage to have a great video! You can use your lovely photos + text + music to create a very compelling slideshow – great for putting in your product pages to explain products or your overall business. If you can though, just pop a short video message from you or a product demo in there to add that extra level of connection. We love Animoto.com for some easy drag and drop slideshow software.

4. Getting video or audio testimonials is a super-effective upgrade from the standard written ones. You can record them via Skype or on your smartphone, or you can even ask your customer to record one of themselves and send it in!

5. One final (slightly random) auditory tip: If you have a physical location where dogs are, try to engineer ways to ensure that when your client walks through the door, or calls you on the phone,

the annoying sound of barking dogs does not negatively impact their experience. This is especially key if they will be leaving their dog with you – you don't want them reminded that their dog might be distressed and barking, or subject to the din of other dogs' barking when they leave! Don't underestimate this one because you think all people with dogs understand that they bark!

In Action:

Ruffwear "My Dog is My" video | YouTube
Check out the "My Dog is My" video on YouTube (just search for it). Check out the STUNNING use of yummy detail imagery and subtle inclusion of product, exemplified by lifestyle, not by explanation. Notice how the music builds to make it all feel more epic (this video makes me get all teary every single time I see it). Also on the Ruffwear YouTube channel are some really practical product explanations – great for supporting their retailers and customers.

8. Touch / Texture

"It was a very conscious decision to make something that felt kind of tactile. We wanted packaging that people wanted to kind of pick up and look at and felt warm and inviting and approachable." – Lucy, Honest Kitchen

This marketing toy is largely used in physical products or spaces, but don't forget its value in our digital world too – by connecting us visually to the tangible. Our Sense of Touch can quickly connect us to our opinions regarding quality.

Even when we can't physically touch something, if we see texture we recognize, we can understand quickly what it feels like and what that means (soft = I want to cuddle into it, sharp = I want to avoid it).

5 Quick and Useful Touch and Texture Tips:

1. Consider in your print materials the impact of touching and holding them. Do you want them to be shiny or matte? Heavy or lightweight? Rounded or edgy? Rectangular, square, or die-cut? You don't have to spend a ton of money to make purposeful choices. If you want "fancy on a budget" use the laminated matte finish (if you're familiar with the original Moo.com cards, they popularized this look/feel). If you want fancy such that cost is no object, consider letterpress or metallic foil. If you want rustic but super cheap, play it up and go for kraft paper or make your OWN with custom rubber stamp of your logo / message.

2. Add some brand textures into your brand guidelines. What are some textures, fabrics, patterns, or surfaces that you can incorporate into your branding? What makes sense for you and your why? Select three to five real, actual textures (things that exist in real life, like wood, sand, snow, metal, flowers, fabric, etc.) and acquire images of them that you can use as backgrounds or fillers in your digital and print materials. This is especially effective as a subtle layer behind solid blocks of color or as little hints or bars alongside very "digital" materials like shopping carts or long web pages. Just make sure the texture you choose makes sense with who and what your brand is all about.

3. If you have packaging or a physical product, be sure to take into consideration the experience of unwrapping or using that product for the first time. Consider if it's on the shelf for a while, how it will wear (will it yellow, peel, or crack?) Is it easy to remove, un-clip, or put back should it not be the right fit? These are opportunities to create positive experiences for your client (or retail client) rather than stressful ones.

4. If you make a product that is pleasant to touch, provide a tester or a swatch book or give away samples of it to encourage clients to experience it for themselves. If touch is a significant part of the experience your customers will have, talk about it – explain how/why you've chosen or created the materials you've used. Let it be a part of your story.

5. In a physical space, don't underestimate the power of furniture and decor textures to give cues to your customer about what kind of business you are – think of the difference between the tile/surroundings in a spa vs. a public bathroom (if you're a groomer you definitely want to be more in the spa category)! Just because your business needs to be dog friendly does not mean it needs to look or feel sterile.

In Action:

P.L.A.Y www.petplay.com | @petplaysf

P.L.A.Y. sells toys and few other little accessories, but is mostly focused on high-quality, beautifully designed dog beds.
They have learned over the years that an important factor in the purchase of their plush beds is that customers can see and touch them. So they created special stickers for retailers to affix to the beds that read "Touch Me" – thus encouraging the customer to engage with the product,

and hopefully, be so enchanted by the softness and obvious comfort, that they purchase it for their pet. P.L.A.Y. also provides their retail stores with swatch books so that customers can touch and experience a wide range of the fabrics that are available. Much easier to pre-sell a product by touch than simply with a photo!

The Labs & Co. thelabsand.co | @thelabsand.co
Another great example from our Working with Dog members! The Labs & Co. are MASTERS of texture. Their obsession with all things pet and their rustic, outdoorsy aesthetic pours through every bit of their marketing and identity. Scroll down their home page or check out their individual portrait sessions to see how they incorporate fur textures into their branding. Check out their blog to see how they designed their header to transform you instantly from laptop to desktop – from digital to the tangible and analog (a great fit for them as they are photographers who shoot a great deal with film). Their Instagram accounts are full of delicious, sense-stimulating textures (sand, word wood, bark, grass, fur, snow, and flowers) that support their wild "why". Also check out their sister instagram: @willowthewildandco

9. Smell / Taste

We are not going to spend as much time on this one, because for most of us, it is quite rare that we get to incorporate the smell and taste senses into our marketing. However, below are some great pet-friendly ways to consider these senses when appealing to the humans who purchase products for them.

3 Quick and Useful Smell and Taste Tips:

1. When selling food items for pets, name your flavors to appeal to humans, since they are the ones who will be choosing for their dog. As a retail store owner I saw this again and again, in nutrition, treats, and novelty items like "dog beer" and "doggy ice cream" – the human picks the flavor that appeals to them.

2. If you have a physical location, much like the sound of barking dogs as discussed previously, your space needs to be absent from the smell of dogs. This is far more critical than you might think. Sense marketing is an entire field, and huge corporations spend a great deal manufacturing scents to fill their spaces in order to entice you to stay longer or purchase more. I can guarantee that NONE of these companies are including the aromas of wet dog or dog pee in their special mix! Put this it at the TOP of your list when making improvements in your business – unpleasant smells imply dirtiness and this will be among the top three reasons that someone will or will not return to your establishment.

3. Food is one of the greatest toys there is! You see this all the time at events and trade shows – and it's not veggies that are on offer! Savvy exhibitors offer free candy to encourage you to come over so they can suck you into conversation and keep you sweet while you chat – plus you feel a little obligated to listen because they've just given you chocolate :)

They are positively reinforcing your behavior – it's simple conditioning! It's no different with the free treats we give dogs at events or in our shops/locations – we want them wagging and pulling their owner in when they walk past our door next time! Simple, cheap, and effective.

In Action:

Planet Dog www.planetdog.com | @planetdoglife
Planet Dog's flagship products are durable, non-toxic, made in the USA "Orbee Tough" rubber toys. In addition to the features I've just mentioned, one of the best things about these toys is that they smell like mint. Yes, really. Not only does this delight the customer (as they imagine their dog's breath improving!) but it also means when you open a box of Orbee toys, or you walk past a display of Orbee toys in a shop, the refreshing smell of mint envelops you. Now I don't know if this solution was meant to cover up a more industrial, less pleasant smell (I mean, think of the smell of new tires) but either way, it's genius. I can tell you from experience that customers do respond positively to it as well! Plus, it is pitched as having the added benefit of freshening your dog's breath - win/win!

10. X-Factor

"37% of U.S. consumers show loyalty to brands that actively support shared causes, such as charities or public campaigns."[14]

This is the domain of the super-marketer (which is now you)! This is the toy that sets the puppies apart from the dogs.

---

14 https://www.accenture.com/us-en/insight-customer-loyalty-gcpr

Get this right and you can almost fail miserably at the other 9. This toy is not number 10 because it's the least important, it just happens to soak into all the other toys. This toy is all about customer experience. All about thrilling your customer, getting them talking, igniting their inner super fan and giving them compelling reasons to pick you over your competition. But you need to know, these are not just tactics to turn off and on; these toys should be integrated heavily into your culture – you need to empower your whole team to deliver and ooze X-Factor. Also, X-Factor is part of a long-term strategy. It is about investing in the future success of your business based on the pleasure quotient of your current customers. It is about relationship-building, customer-service mastering and especially, happy-making.

Spoiler Alert: X-Factor is essentially your Marketing Sense #6 which you'll learn all about shortly, so there's a bit of repeat, but the X-Factor sense often has some significant visual representation, or should be mentioned, referenced or utilized in the physical / aesthetic side of your brand, so I will briefly mention it here. For the tips below, think of ways to incorporate them into the aesthetics of your marketing materials.

5 Quick and Useful X-Factor Tips:

1. If you are most compelled by a particular charitable or social cause, build your business around it. Be all about it. Eat, sleep, and breathe it. Not for PR, not because it's trendy, but because if you won the lottery, this is how you'd spend your time and other resources. You don't have to be a charitable business to contribute to a cause – you can be for-profit and still help. How you do that is up to you but you will need to have a very clear mission. Customers will respond and support your conviction passionately. This is important to talk about in your marketing and sales materials.

2. This one might seem obvious, but it is too important not to mention: Package yourself or your product immaculately. If you are your product – your physical appearance is part of your marketing. If you have a physical product, the way it is packaged, tagged, boxed, and sent out all have a huge impact on your customer's experience. This is how you walk your talk. Don't spend all your profit on this (which is easy to do!) but consider it carefully and craft this part of your customer's journey with care. Create process around packaging so it is consistent. Take photos of it and encourage customers to do the same so that it organically becomes part of your desire-building on social media (you can even get influencers to do an #unboxing for you). If you are your product, take the time and effort to consistently show up as the brand your customer has invested in – from head to toe.

3. This one is fun, easy, and feels good. Surprise and delight your clients at every opportunity. Give them generous gifts (this is most effective when you begin to understand the lifetime value of your client so you know just how generous you can afford to be long-term – but this works better the bigger you go! I'm talking free iPads and weekends away (barring specific bribery laws in your particular industry). Provide them special privileges or access to things they desire that money can't buy. Don't charge them for extras when they're fully expecting to pay. Go out of your way to do the unreasonably, amazingly thoughtful. Send them a handwritten note. Be a friendly, thoughtful human. This is the most direct and simple way to build two of your most powerful routes to future business: return customers and word of mouth!

4. Another hugely compelling element of X-Factor is increasing ease, accessibility, and convenience. Smooth out the resistance wherever it exists. Do the work to flatten out wrinkles in your product, packaging, software, communication, delivery, and other avenues that massively impact your customers' ability to interact with you or your product. It is YOUR JOB to understand what they want and to make it as easy as physically possible. Think Amazon. Think Apple. Go beyond what is normal or acceptable to blow your customers' mind. Put the work in to beat the status quo in your industry. You will reap the rewards.

5. One final tip that I think is a great way for entrepreneurs to implement X-Factor is to encourage social media use as a customer service tool. Pick the platform(s) you and your team are most comfortable with and invite your customers to meet you there. Twitter and Facebook are both fantastic for this – it can be slightly harder for you to track, but that's your problem – not theirs. You're then living #2 and making it easy for them to get in touch. You are meeting them where they are, not putting them on hold on the phone or letting their issues disappear into your inbox abyss. You are acting like a human. Equally, if you search, especially on Twitter, You might find people who have issues you didn't even know existed, and if you show up there and solve them, you become a serious hero. Again, make it clear in your marketing and sales materials that people can reach you on social media instead of using the phone or email.

In Action:

Dog is Good   www.dogisgood.com | @dogisgood
When I was actively involved as Creative Director at Dog is Good I was extremely passionate about this element of our business.

Some little things we did included making the tags on our tees also stickers, sending the occasional free gift with orders, even printing little surprise messages inside the neck of our tees so that after your purchase you found a little something extra to make you smile. My partners John and Gila were religious about being easy to do business with and still maintain that as a pillar of the Dog is Good legacy. These elements of "surprise and delight" were definitely at the heart of our growth over the first eight to 10 years of business.

That's It!

That's the end of our Marketing Toy Box, and if you're feeling like, "Whew, that was a load of info," don't sweat it. You don't need to memorize and implement all of that right at this moment. Dog-ear the page and come back to it when you're designing something new or need a bit of advice about a project. These tools I just have to share with you, because I feel like leaving them out is a disservice to you, but I don't expect that you'll take it in all at once and magically become an expert. Next, I'd love to give you tool to keep all those marketing toys organized...

Brand Guidelines

Once you've determined what your Brands Marketing Toys are, it's helpful to group them together in some sort of document. Guidelines are very helpful to maintain consistency when you need to create new marketing materials.

This is especially true when you need to outsource tasks to staff, designers, or developers. If you have brand guidelines, you will exponentially increase the chances that whatever it is that they create looks, feels, and works right for you and your customer. No more re-inventing the wheel each time – you want your brand to look and feel the same everywhere it shows up!

If you hire a professional to do your logo or brand identity, very often they will include a simple brand guidelines document which outlines your logo usage, color palette, and fonts. It is worth asking at the beginning of the project if this will be included. This helpful tool is usually worth paying a bit more for. If you haven't had a professional logo designed, or have used a service like 99designs.com, you can DIY your own brand guidelines.

We created a robust resource to help you do this over at workingwithdog.com/brand-guidelines.

15. Sense Five: Sense of Smell

Ok, so we now know why we do what we do, and who we do it for. We've established guidelines for the ways our messages and products show up in our marketing materials. Now we need to crank up the desire factor so that when our potential customers happen upon us, they stay. They hangout and then they buy.

What Is It?

You know that moment when you're walking down the city street, or through a fair or market and suddenly the intoxicating scent of warming sugar (where are the waffles?) or baking bread (Subway is great at this) or some other delicious food aroma floats in to your nostrils? Suddenly, whether you were hungry or not, you must have the thing that you just got a whiff of! Our fifth Marketing Sense, Sense of Smell, is all about that. Not literally about smell (although you'll see an example later of how one MDDB actually does use smell to add desirability to their dog toys). This sense is about building intense desire, which then leads to purchase. So far in our other Marketing Senses, we've covered your why, who, what, and where... this one is part one of your "how."

Why Does It Matter?

Why does desire matter? Think about any romantic relationship you've ever had... how long would it last if in the beginning there was no desire? No lust? No fireworks? For your sake, I hope not long! We humans are a species of expert hedonists – we are pleasure seekers. Brands are pleasure delivery systems. It's what we do. We are desire ninjas.

This sense is all about setting the stage to get that first yes from a new customer. This first conversion is critical because statistically, the second yes is much easier to get than the first one. This sense is the art of making it a no brainer to buy from you, no matter what your prices are. This is the front line of revenue creation; the moment where investing in building a brand really starts to pay dividends. Where instead of having to convince someone to please, please buy something, they wait in line to have the privilege of owning a "your brand" original.

"A dog leash used to be a commodity. It's a red nylon thing to keep your dog from running away. We wanted to make sure that it wasn't that. Why couldn't your dog's leash be an extension of your lifestyle just like the shoes you're wearing or your purse, or your watch? It could be and it should be an extension of your personal style. If I'm going out and I'm all in black and I want my dog's leash to be black as well and if my girlfriend is wearing leopard shoes, maybe her dog leash should have the leopard print too. I think with that mentality, we ended up hitting the sweet spot in the global niche. And that's one of the reasons why we grew so quickly, not just in Brazil. Because every dog owner in the world felt the desire for having cool pet products" - Thad, Zee.Dog

"Be the Fox Pee."
@workingwithdog

How Does It Show Up?

Do you know what smell is supposedly the MOST impossible for a dog to ignore? The one that makes them absolutely go mental when they catch a sniff of it? The one they cannot and will not walk past without inhaling, rolling in, or peeing on? It's fox pee. It's doggy catnip. If your customers are the dog, you want to be the fox pee. You want to be absolutely impossible to resist. In this process, great brands end up creating a manic almost obsessive level of enthusiasm (remember the Dogvergnügen tattoo I mentioned?) When your customers are tattooing your artwork on their body, you know you've nailed your Marketing Senses and have become the fox pee!

To show up as fox pee, you'll need to do two things:
1. Create desire
2. Eliminate friction

Each of these stages is made up of some absolutely critical skills that brands are experts in and many businesses don't bother with. Why? Well some of them are difficult to measure, most of them take time to master, and they're not automatic or obvious to most entrepreneurs when they're starting out. Some of these skills even make life harder, but they matter to brands because they believe in something bigger than just revenue:

"We make life quite difficult for ourselves sometimes with the product values and the things that we put in place, in terms of sourcing: No ingredients at all from China, using humanely raised, free-range meats, that are free of antibiotics, and added growth hormones, paying extra for chickens that are lucky enough to have eucalyptus branches put in their enclosures so they have an enriched environment versus being raised in squalor in intense factory farming conditions.

We do all of those things because we believe they're important and those are the stores we tell about what we're doing and why. We take a bit of responsibility for educating people and attempting to raise the bar in the industry at large when it comes to pet food. Ultimately, it just comes back to acting in a way that people trust us to act in... and doing a good job of storytelling." - Lucy, Honest Kitchen

How to Master Part 1 of the "How" Sense

Before we learn how to action this Sense of Smell, I want you to close your eyes for a moment and think briefly about the best things you've ever purchased. They don't have to be "things" - they can be experiences... but they have to be memorable. Indulgent things you HAD to have... maybe you saved up to buy them, maybe you bought them on a whim, maybe you even felt guilty at first but then were SO glad you spent on them because they ended up being worth every penny in pure pleasure or reliable utility.

Think back to the moment you fell in love with these things - the moment you knew that one day you would purchase them. Why did you desire them so fiercely? What ticked that electric box in your brain that said, "She will be mine, oh yes, she will be mine." (Wayne's World reference, yes I am a child of the '80s – #sorrynotsorry.)

I'd be willing to bet that somewhere along the line between knowing these delicious things or services existed, and actually purchasing them, you bought into a story. You believed something about the product or the brand that makes the product. There was something irresistible about its role in your life, about what it says about you that you own it, about why it's a superior thing or about the tremendous value this thing would bring to your life.

Is it limited edition? Is it handmade? Is it so exceptionally beautiful that it brings you joy every time you see it, touch it, or use it? Is it eco-friendly? Does it have a one-of-a-kind story? Does it represent a place or time in your life that you want to cherish? Did you meet the person who made it? Are you enamored with the brand who thought to craft something so perfectly suited to your exact taste? Does it make you feel special, wealthy, healthy, whole, beautiful, smart, trendy, cultured, skilled, generous, or generally just good about yourself, your life, your work, or your home? Is it proof that you belong to a certain "club"?

These are all very important questions to ask yourself – to understand how you feel about the brands and things you love. This is how a Million Dollar Brand optimizes this fifth sense: it understands what feelings its customers and fans wants to feel, stirs them up, and then presents itself as the physical manifestation of that pleasure, or solution to that pain.

Exercise: Have a look back at your notes from Sense 2, where we dove into the fears and desires of your who. Do a bit of brainstorming or free writing about what your avatars are thinking and feeling. What kinds of conversations are they having about these feelings? What ways do your products or services ease their pain? What ways do your products or services bring immense pleasure into their day or life?

1. Create Delicious Desire

"We were really looking for products that were undiscovered, especially in toys. We want character and some attitude. My co-founder, Carley, did a lot of that; went to some of the pet shows, met a lot of vendors... it's one of those things when you see even just the packaging and the story behind it, we say "Yeah, that's us, and we get it." It matches up with who we are" – Matt, BarkBox

The first magical desire-creating aspect of your Sense of Smell is pieced together by mastering the first four marketing senses, and one important skill: **storytelling.**

A. Optimize Senses 1-4

So far in this book we've learned how and why to:

1. **Lead with why**

2. **Speak specifically to your who** and no one else

3. **Ensure that what your offering is what your who wants and are willing to pay for**

4. **Invest in compelling, consistent communication** touchpoints where your who can fall in love

Now we're going to actively woo them.

"Building a brand is not easy. To this day the smartest investment we have made was to spend the time, not just money, but to spend the time to think about what kind of story we want to tell. The market is saturated, but there's always room for innovation in both products and branding that create experiences. These brand experiences start with the stories brands tell. For us the message has evolved over time, but the core message has always been that we want to make products that are better for pets, but also for people and the planet. We want to make impactful products that can change people's lives." – Will, P.L.A.Y.

B. Tell Stories

There are words... and then are whispers... conspiracies, divine messages, urban legends, captivating narratives... all of which lead us on a journey and leave us desperate to know the resolution... the next twist. There are websites... and then there are online experiences... portals to curated worlds, where the click of a mouse can transport you to a heaven of delicious lines, colors, words, and images that reinforce what you want to believe to be true about yourself and the world.

There is copy... and then there are stories.

The difference? One is straight-laced, no-nonsense, logical, and practical... the other is enchanting, sensual, addicting, and transformational. The tiny thread separating the two? Emotions.

Emotional Connections.

Yup, once again I am banging on about the importance of connecting emotionally with your people. Not logically, not with common sense and facts, but with real, raw, vulnerable, captivating and compelling emotional content. We're talking storytelling, people.

"We're not just a seller of product; we are a brand with a story. Our biggest goal is to continue to tell and grow that story in order to sell the brand. You know, I think some companies out there have it a little bit easier because they are just selling a toy or they are just selling collars and leaches all day long; that's all they do. But were selling a story because we have several products that really translate to the lifestyle that people share with their dogs."
– Stephanie, Planet Dog

The Two Rules for Storytelling

Great stories rattle your cage. They make you weep, dance, smile, laugh, phone a friend... they get under your skin and inside you. They move you. The very best stories are memorable: a hero's journey, star-crossed lovers, urban legends – they have classic narratives that we can remember, repeat, and relate to. As for storytelling for your business, well then there is the added element of falling in love with the storyteller. You.

There is a lot of talk these days about storytelling as a part of branding or marketing. I am sure you have heard more than once that you need to be telling stories in your business, but what does that actually MEAN and HOW do you actually DO it?

Well we've established the two rules of great storytelling:

1. Connecting emotionally
2. Being memorable.

Sounds simple enough, but like most kinds of "simple" it is much, much harder to create something simple than it is to just create something that "works." Simple is refined, elegant, edited, and direct. Simple is distilling down 100 ideas to the three that matter. Simple is bullet points instead of paragraphs. Simple is empty space and silence instead of filling every square inch with noise. Simple is one product, one image, or one statement instead of five. Simple takes intention, confidence, and clarity. So that's where we start...

Intention

You're probably sick of me hearing by now that you have to start with "why" but it's not ever going to be any less true, so if we're going to continue to be friends, you might as well embrace it!

When setting out to tell a story in or for your business, you don't have to know how it's going to turn out, what words you're going to use, or how the twists will turn. But you do need to know three things:

1. **What is the desired outcome**: How do you want your audience to think, feel or act as a result?

2. **What is the takeaway message:** What is the one thing you want them to remember?

3. **Where does this story fit in with your brand?** Have a consistent voice and consistent theme.

Confidence

Babbling, over-filling and indecision are the hallmarks of insecurity. It's fine to be insecure about things – boy aren't we all – but it's not compelling to show up that way in your stories. Fight the urge to try to say it all, show it all, cover it all in every story you tell. Fight the urge to over-explain – let things just linger out there and let your audience fill in some of the blanks for themselves. The worst thing you can do is tell a compelling, thought-provoking, interesting story, and then summarize it at the end and explain the nuances of the metaphors you've used – no! Take the risk of letting people interpret for themselves your words. A little mystery, a little flight of fancy is OK now and then! But this does bring me to clarity.

Clarity

While you don't want your stories to be prescriptive and so straightforward there's no magic, emotion or angst, you don't want to clutter them up with big words your audience doesn't know with too many syllables that make sentences tough to decipher or too many conflicting concepts or products fighting to be the hero.

Most often, I find clarity comes through a combination of intention (being clear for yourself what the intention of the story is before you tell it) and editing. Restraint is a HUGE part of clarity – resisting the urge to try to be everything to everyone, and sell everything all at the same time. Notice, once again, I haven't said a thing about selling, but clarity can be the difference between making that intention a reality and just telling an interesting story that does nothing for your brand or business. Clarity is where you "bring it back around" and make it clear to your audience the way your story relates to their exact need and their exact desires. How do you relate to your clients' exact desires and needs? Clarity! You know first of all, who they are, and second of all, what those needs and desires ARE, and thirdly, what language to use to talk to them. (If you haven't done this – be sure to check out this article and the corresponding challenge to help you get clarity around your ideal client!)

In Action

Now I realize if storytelling doesn't come naturally to you – this all seems a bit abstract. That's ok – just like any other skill you've mastered in your life, becoming an expert storyteller takes time, dedication, and care. Of course like most skills your business needs, you can outsource the storytelling of your brand. Most of us hire storytellers all the time (which as we discussed in Sense 4, is sometimes the best route): designers, copywriters, photographers, editors etc. But I do recommend that you learn the basics and you keep flexing these storytelling muscles.

Ultimately you are the soul of your business – and when the day comes for that big interview or that brilliant guest post opportunity, you want to have the practice in so you can connect emotionally with your audience and be memorable.

The best thing you can do is keep crafting stories to find your voice and practice connecting emotionally and being memorable: on your social posts, in blogs, on web pages, and in person. For more support we have a whole module for members over at workingwithdog.com/storytelling/.

2. Eliminate Friction

"Where there is friction there is opportunity. Either solve it for your customers today, or your competitor will tomorrow."
- Brian Eisenberg

Once you've stoked that desire, it's time to pave the way to a transaction, an easy yes. I call the obstacles between your customers and their first purchase "friction points." If you have an existing business, you will know what the friction points are already, because you will have received feedback or engaged in unpleasant conversations repeatedly over the same subjects. Usually, these points have to do with price, availability, terms, convenience (hours, delivery, wait times) and other realities in our business dampen the overall experience of our customer.

Many of these friction points will be difficult to resolve, some of them impossible because that's the nature of the service or product, but many of them will simply come down to not meeting your customers' exceptions. Some of these expectations may seem wildly unfair, but think about it this way... wouldn't you rather buy the best product at the best price and get it immediately? Of course! We want it all! We can't expect our customers to want something different than we do, can we?

Our job is to do the best we can to give our people the impossible. To tackle the "industry standard price" by finding a new method of production, by believing in our product enough to stand by a money-back guarantee that never expires, or to conquer logistical nightmares to offer free next-day shipping (ahem, Amazon). Any time we can deliver the impossible we are eliminating friction. Our customer doesn't know it's impossible; they don't care what we have to go through to make it happen, but they do appreciate it immensely when we do. That is when buying from us becomes a no-brainer.

There are essentially two levers to pull to make this happen:

1. Deliver great value
2. Make it easy to buy

We'll start by diving into why it is value and not price that matters, and then we'll discuss how to clear distractions and obstacles so your customer can take that value straight to checkout without a second thought!

1. Value

"The philosophy behind the brand really is making the best pet product in the world with super, super affordable pricing. We don't believe that pet products need to be expensive and they shouldn't. I think they need to always be top-quality because there are a lot of safety issues when you're talking about someone's dog, but how much are people willing to pay? We wanted to make sure that the pricing was right from the beginning but the quality didn't suffer."
– Thad, Zee.Dog

"First and foremost, we never really looked at price because there were a lot of dog products that were on the market. I could buy a dog pack that was sold in a flat plastic bag for $15. The problem is that this product, when it was actually out in the environment that they're intended for, didn't hold up. When we start to build a product, we build it to satisfy or to address a specific need. Then later in the game, we try to figure out how to make that affordable."
– Patrick, Ruffwear

"Feedback that we got regarding the QR code tag was, "Why don't you have a phone number for those folks who don't know what it is?" And so we did; we put a 24-7 call center in and we actually decided to make that free. Nobody else does it for free. Everyone else charges for their call center, but we said well, you know, our purpose is to get these pets home fast and to make it so that people don't have to think. It becomes a no-brainer about putting this tag on their pet, so the money won't be an issue if they can't afford to pay a monthly service, they don't have to." – Lorien, PetHub

"We're constantly looking at areas where we could introduce maybe an organic alternative, or an additional animal welfare component when it comes to the meats or the fish. But it definitely is a matter of also trying to balance cost. As an example, I think our celery is around $4/lb. but if we were to go into organic dehydrated celery, that would be $12 or $13 a pound. So if we plug that into our formula cost, that's going to make the finished product unaffordable for almost everybody. There is a bit of common sense that has to come in to balancing value for us and for the customer."
- Lucy, Honest Kitchen

When your customers are making their mind up about whether or not to buy from you, price is only one part of the equation. As business owners, we obsess over price (which is understandable as it is the friction point we hear about most often) and of course price is an integral part of marketing. But really, it's value we should be concerned with. Value is the context that gives price meaning. If I say to you, "That cost me $5000," you don't know whether that's cheap or outrageously expensive until you know what it is that I bought! 5k for a house? Bargain! 5k for a meal? Ouch!

No matter what you do, what your prices are, or whether you consider yourself to be a low-price brand or a premium one, you want your customers to feel like they're getting a good deal. This is an especially tricky skill to master as this feeling varies so greatly from customer to customer, and you personally might have a very different attitude towards money or value than your ideal client does. I should say again that the best way to determine what is good value for your clients is to ask them. As entrepreneurs, we go on gut feel a lot of times, which is really effective for some decisions, but the only way we know for sure if our assumptions are correct is to collect data. We'll be talking about that a bit in the final sense, Part 2 of your "how," but I wanted to mention it now so we are all on the same page. Now, let's dive in to three ways to create value for your customer, to increase their desire, to purchase: anchoring, selling the experience, and being generous.

A) Anchor

Earlier we discussed price anchoring when we discussed diving your products up into novelty, core and premium options. This is one way to embed the feeling of "good value" into your offering. By giving people an easy yes, very cheap option and the very high-cost option, the middle option suddenly seems less expensive and you feel good about your choice.

B) Sell the Experience

One of the best ways to side-step someone's judgement about whether or not your product is expensive is to sell more than just the thing. This tactic is just for brands, because businesses just can't pull it off. You, the brand builder, have the chance to sell not just the lead or harness, but the perfect dog walk: One where you can even hold a latte in your free hand and squirrel-or-no-squirrel, you'll be able to enjoy the great outdoors and no one is coming home with second degree coffee burns. You have the chance to not just sell doggy daycare, but a safe, enriching experience where dogs get a dose of massage, training, and socialization that they just can't get anywhere else, and humans get peace of mind. You get where I am going with this? Experiences are priceless. Feeling great about yourself as a wonderful caretaker of your pets is priceless. Things can be compared against one another and judged accordingly; the intangible emotions and moments that go with them cannot. Sell experiences. Sell stories. Sell feelings and moments. The real value in any product or service is in the experience they provide or the problem they solve, so use that to your advantage when building desire.

C) Be Generous

If you've been in business for a few years, no matter what you sell, it's very likely that you've gotten very used to hearing complaints about cost or price. For many entrepreneurs, this repeated conversation can lead to defensiveness about price and policies, which can often lead into a downward spiral of fear-based beliefs rooted in "not enough." This is absolutely toxic to your brand. If you find yourself feeling defensive when a customer wants or expects something, and you're sick of explaining why they can't have it or why it costs more, you need to stop and consider what you're defending.

It may be time to really listen to that feedback and consider ways you might be able to give them what they want. What if you could generously just hand over what they want? What would you need in return to make it viable? Here's the reality – if you won't, someone else will. You will be stuck in the background complaining about how the new guy doesn't know how it's done and the new guy will be laughing all the way to the bank.

I am not suggesting that we should just give every customer what they want for the price they want, but what I am suggesting is that you take the time to look at your business and your products from your customers' point of view and ask yourself, "What would I want if I were going to buy this thing? What would make a no-brainer to say yes?" If you can operate from that customer-centric position, rather than what your job title, industry, or the last 20 years of tradition tell you should be done, you will be creating real value and you will finally find the demand you've been looking for.

This is all about the Dogly Principle of generosity. Be generous with your customers; give them what they want. You need boundaries so you know what your business needs to make the transaction viable, but start from the customers' needs and work backwards to make it work, not the other way around. In addition to the obvious benefits of building desire (getting more sales), when the product you're offering is generous, you will make those customers so happy that you're making it easy and painless. They will reward you with repeat purchases and referral business.

Exercise: Value Proposition
To keep this whole value concept front and center, many brands will come up with what they call a "value proposition." You can have one for the overall company, but what I think is more effective is one for each product category.

This value proposition is a practical way to ensure that your products are meeting the promises that your brand is continually making, and that the Dogly Principles and others standards you set for quality and consistency are being met when you develop something new. Equally, writing this down for each new product or category will give you a great tool to use when marketing that product: writing the product description, talking about it in the media, creating signage or ads, etc. Sometimes if you don't keep the experience or feeling you're selling at the top of your mind, you may find yourself simply describing and selling the thing instead, which makes it much harder to show value.

Example: At Dog is Good we were constantly creating new pieces of apparel to screen print our designs on. When we first started, we'd have to source and purchase these "blanks" from apparel companies – which presented a wide range of options, restrictions, qualities, prices, cuts, and minimums. We often had difficulty deciding which pieces to use in our line because there were just SO many to choose from, many of which we really liked, but some of which were not the right price or range of sizing for our who. Once we picked these pieces, we'd then have to pick the color palette for the new season of designs so these different items could be merchandised well together in a shop.

There were so many decisions to be made along the way, both for the end user and the retailer, relating to the product itself and the price we could deliver it for, that we felt like we were starting from scratch each time. Eventually, we finally came up with some exacting standards for what these pieces HAD to be to be included in our line. Not only did this help our decision-making, but it also helped us communicate to the customer all the steps that went into a Dog is Good tee shirt that made it the perfect product.

Dog is Good: Exacting Standards

- ○ Fashion
- ○ Fit
- ○ Originality
- ○ Affordability
- ○ Comfort

In addition to these product-specific standards, we wrap everything we do up in our why: how good it feels to be with Dog. So our product descriptions would include a lot more of that than anything else. We saved the technical descriptions about the material, care instructions and fit for the fine print at the bottom. Generally, by the time people looked at the technical information, they were already sold on the tee and they just needed to know what size to buy.

2. Make it Easy

"94% of customers who have a low-effort service experience will buy from that same company again."[15]

The next half of eliminating friction for your customer is possibly the most obvious thing I'll mention in this entire book, but sadly one of the most overlooked: Just make it easy for them to buy from you. It sounds pretty simple, but I cannot even NAME the number of times I have heard Pet Parents talk about trying to hire a dog walker or dog trainer or groomer and never even getting a call or an email back.

---

[15] http://blog.accessdevelopment.com/index.php/2013/11/the-ultimate-collection-of-loyalty-statistics

We have all had poor retail experiences where the website doesn't work or we don't receive confirmation, or in a physical shop, we can't get good help, can't pay with credit card, or feel otherwise unwanted or underserved. How tragic! You have done ALL THAT WORK to get someone to your website or in to your physical location. Do not fail them in the final moment before purchase! There is NOTHING more important than this. Nothing you're spending your time on is more critical than ensuring that the people who want to buy from you can do so easily. If you build the most exquisite brand with the most moving "why" and the most gorgeous products but no one can figure out how to check out from your online shop, you've failed. Remember when I said earlier that building a brand is not an excuse for not doing the work? This is part of that. The way you treat your customers and how easy and pleasant it is for them to buy from you are far more defining features of your brand than your logo or tagline. If you've worked through this book and have nailed every other section but see an epic to-do list coming out of this one, stop and work through that list before moving on. This is simply too critical to ignore, and all the promises I've made to you about the MDDB Advantage Cycle and your dreams coming true are on the other side of getting this right.

"Have we made a product that can be easily merchandised? Have we thought about a display? Most stores can't possibly carry too many beds simply because of space limitations, so can we be innovative? Instead of forcing high minimums on retailers, can we come up with some sort of fulfilment program which will encourage stores to stock a few pieces of our items, and have things like a swatch book and product showcase sheets where all the bed designs are very clearly and visually displayed, so when a customer likes a certain bed but they want a different size, the store can order it for them? Things that basically make it easy for retailers to be successful with our line." – Will, P.L.A.Y.

"Make it Easy" Audit:

To help, here is a quick 10-question audit for you to use to assess where you're at now in terms of being easy to do business with. This will help you identify areas for improvement.

Prioritize these improvements above all else!

1. Where do people buy from you?

2. In each place, how do people actually pay you?
> Have you received feedback about any of these payment points? Is there any way you can add or remove options to make it easier or reduce steps?

3. Can someone purchase something from you online at 2am?
> If no, would it be possible in some way add this option, even if it's a gift certificate or a "package" or you may have to refund them later if they're not a good fit?

4. What are the typical steps between someone knowing they want to buy from you and actually receiving the thing or service?
> Have you received feedback about this process? Is there any way you can remove steps to make it faster or easier for someone to give you money?

5. How many ways are listed on your website to get ahold of you?
> You should have two at a minimum and at least one of them should be an email or phone number

6. What is the average length of time they will wait to hear from you via each method?
> If any of these are more than 24 hours, eliminate it, outsource it or automate it so that people get a quicker response.

7. What are the social media platforms you list as ways to interact with you?

8. Which of these are monitored on a daily basis?
> If you list platforms like Facebook, Twitter, or Instagram which have a message option and you're not ever present there, you need to choose to either show up consistently or ditch them. If people are getting in touch with you and you're not paying attention, this is very harmful to their experience and to your brand.

9. Do you have your customers or clients sign a contract? If so, how is it delivered / signed/ received?
> If you're still using paper, it's time to consider an upgrade to digital forms (or both). No one has time to print and scan anymore. This can be a big obstacle between you and getting paid!

10. Do you currently have a follow-up email, questionnaire, or survey that you ask your customers to take to get feedback after their purchase?
> We'll discuss this more in the next sense, but this is a 100% must.

HINT: If you run a dog service business (walking, sitting, training, photography, transport, wellness etc.) you need to check out BookYourPet.com. This is a pet-exclusive software that you can drop into your own website to allow people to book appointments online. You can choose to approve appointments as they come in or let people book in automatically; customers receive text confirmations and easy directions, they can pay you online or in person, you can send photos of their pet during the service, and they can provide reviews after the fact. It's EPIC and it's FREE. There is also a mobile app. It's the best thing for "make it easy" that I've ever seen for service businesses!

18. Sense Six: Sense of Taste

We are at the very end of our Marketing Senses. We've gotten all the way to the point where our who has purchased. Hooray, transactions! Now because we're a brand and not just a business, it's very likely that our customer will purchase again and tell friends. This sense is about facilitating that process and making it easy for them.

What Is It?

They've purchased. They're in. They've taken a big ol' bite out of the value you've offered. Now: is the taste lingering in their mouth sweet or sour? This Sense of Taste is Part 2 of your "how." This sense is all about how you will show up post-purchase to ensure your customers do two very important things. The first is to come back; to purchase again. The second is to share. Tell a friend, spread the word. These critical final touches in your brand experience should be as well considered as your why, your pricing, and your website because of the significant impact they can have on our MDDB Advantage Cycle: creating demand, profitability, and influence.

Why Does It Matter and How Does It Show Up?

"Right now, there is a fortune in word of mouth that can be created for companies who nurture relationships in small but meaningful ways that turn customers into vocal brand advocates across large social media networks." – Gary Vaynerchuk

Ensuring that taste in your customers mouth is a sweet one leads to two very desirable behaviors:

1. Repeat purchase
2. Positive word of mouth

You are a very savvy person; I am not sure I even need to explain why repeat purchases and word of mouth matters, do I? How about if I just give you some mind-boggling stats?

Repeat Purchase

- Increasing customer retention by 5% can lead to a 25% - 95% increase in profit.[16]
- A repeat customer spends 67% more than a new one.[17]
- The average online conversion rate is somewhere between 1% and 3%... but a repeat customer has a 60% – 70% chance of converting.
- After one purchase, a customer has a 27% chance of returning to your store. However, if you can get that customer to come back and make a second and third

---

16 https://hbr.org/2000/07/e-loyalty-your-secret-weapon-on-the-web

17 http://blog.accessdevelopment.com/index.php/2013/11/the-ultimate-collection-of-loyalty-statistics

purchase, they have a 54% chance of making another purchase.[18]

- ○ 40% of an ecommerce store's revenue is created by 8% of its customers.[19]
- ○ 1% of a retail website's users generate as much as 40% of its revenue.[20]
- ○ On average, loyal customers are worth up to 10x as much as their first purchase.[21]

Word of Mouth

- ○ 82% of marketers use word-of-mouth marketing to increase their brand awareness, but 43% expect word-of-mouth marketing to improve their direct sales.[22]
- ○ 64% of marketing executives indicated that they believe word of mouth is the most effective form of marketing.[23]
- ○ When someone shares or talks about a brand on social media, there's a significant correlation to purchasing behavior.[24]

---

18 https://www.sweettoothrewards.com/blog/repeat-customers-profitable-stats-to-prove/

19http://success.adobe.com/assets/en/downloads/whitepaper/13926.digital_index_loyal_shoppers_report.pdf

20 http://www.socialannex.com/blog/2016/02/05/ultimate-customer-loyalty-statistics-2016/

21 http://www.socialannex.com/blog/2016/02/05/ultimate-customer-loyalty-statistics-2016/

22 https://www.getambassador.com/blog/word-of-mouth-marketing-statistics

23 American Marketing Association (AMA)

24 http://www.business2community.com/marketing/numbers-dont-lie-2016-nielsen-study-revealed-referrals-01477256#uGYUeB5mhhPi8RJw.99

- ○ The vast majority (more than 80%) of Americans seek recommendations when making a purchase of any kind.[25]
- ○ 55% of U.S. consumers express loyalty by recommending the brands and companies they love to family friends.[26]

And how about this doozy including BOTH repeat purchase AND word of mouth...

"The number of people a customer refers your site to increases with the number of purchases they have made. Each time a customer makes a purchase, they are becoming more comfortable with you, and thus are more willing to make a positive referral.[27]"

* drops mic and walks off stage*

Return Clients

It is far less expensive to get a customer to buy again than to go get a new customer to purchase. Less cost means more potential for profit. I like profit. How about you? Repeat customers convert at a higher rate, spend more over time and are more comfortable supplying you with those all-important word-of-mouth referrals. What's not to like?

25 http://www.business2community.com/marketing/numbers-dont-lie-2016-nielsen-study-revealed-referrals-01477256#uGYUeB5mhhPi8RJw.99

26 http://blog.accessdevelopment.com/index.php/2013/11/the-ultimate-collection-of-loyalty-statistics

27 http://www.bain.com/Images/Value_online_customer_loyalty_you_capture.pdf

Word of Mouth

"Brands that inspire a higher emotional intensity receive 3x as much word of mouth as less emotionally-connected brands. The same academic study also found that highly differentiated brands earn more positive word-of-mouth.[28]"

Do you know what a "higher emotional intensity" brand is? It's one that is passionate and connects emotionally with its who. Do you know what a "highly differentiated brand" is? It's one that STANDS OUT. It's one that has optimized its Marketing Senses, knows who it is and why it does what it does and it proudly yells about it all over the place. Apparently, people LIKE IT when you're passionate, connect emotionally, and are confident! Who knew?

So basically, by skipping this one sense you could be missing out on 99% of the stuff that helps your business grow organically. Let's decode the word "organically" for a second; in this case I mean without paying dearly for it. I mean #FREE.

How to Master Part 1 of the "How" Sense

It's nearly impossible to give you the secrets to the art and science behind repeat customers and word of mouth in just a few pages of this book. It's a craft that marketers have been researching and debating for over 50 years. The reality is that no one really knows for sure, but there is one theme that stands out as an effective strategy to help you master Part 2 of this "how" sense, and that is to build relationships.

---

28 https://www.getambassador.com/blog/word-of-mouth-marketing-statistics

Build Relationships

"I think that the natural way that a company would've been built, even 10 years ago, would be that a company's competency would be built around function. We would be good at box fulfilment and merchandising around the subscription model. After dog, we'd want to replicate that with cat, and then fish and then snake and then just keep coming... but I think the change that's happened, largely driven by technology and the consumer, is that our competency now is much more around the relationships. Relationships we have with the consumer and the brand we're building and being authentic in that. We are our own audience, we love our dogs, we connect to them.

"We know as a result, the subscription box isn't the only thing we can offer. We now have BarkPost, which is a media and entertainment property and we see about 10 or 11 million unique visitors to that a month, and we've opened our shop and we have events and there's more and more and more coming. We feel that the dog-obsessed person is wildly underserved and we feel we can connect to that audience in a really genuine way, so we will continue to do that." – Matt, BarkBox

Focusing time and resources on properly building relationships with your customers is a somewhat controversial choice. Like Matt mentions, the old-school way to build a business is to build competencies and then duplicate them in different markets. However, in the world we live in now, the most valuable thing in your business may be your brand, relationships, and email list – valuable resources that will not show up on your balance sheet!

Businesses don't necessarily invest in building relationships for the sake of it because the direct results are hard to measure and because not all customers in all industries actually want a relationship with the brands they interact with. Truly excelling at relationship-building requires letting go a bit and choosing to show up as a brand. As a friend. As a human who, like in the BarkBox example above, connects with their audience because they are their audience; they are 100% authentic (ahem Dogly Principles) in their interactions because they are loving what they're doing. Then, the relationships come easily.

Getting this sense right requires thinking more like a human than a business. Humans crave connection. Let the love of why you do what you do flow freely and soak into every square inch of your brand and be the bond that connects you with your customers, team members, and partners. Here are a few practical ways to pull that off:

1. Live the Dogly Principles
2. Listen and engage
3. Build a brand-based culture
4. Surprise and delight
5. Build relationships with partners and influencers

1. Live the Dogly Principles

At the beginning of the book I introduced you to the Dogly Principles:

1. Generosity (and boundaries)
2. Simplicity
3. Authenticity
4. Consistency
5. Quality

I mentioned that if the Six Marketing Senses are the roadmap; these principles are the rules of the road. Previously, I mentioned that these principles are designed to build "know, like, and trust" - which is another way of saying "relationships." Follow these commandments and great relationships are a likely consequence.

2. Listen and Engage

"It's interesting; the smaller stores tend to be better because they have a more one-on-one relationship with their customer. They know them by name, they know their dogs, they know their dog's individual issues. Our product is one that is a high-education piece. Small retailers that love our products and sell quite a bit, but it's not the big boon that we thought it would be. It wasn't until we dug in and started listening to our customers about the retail customer and the consumer that we realized that, oh, this isn't the best channel for us. Everything that I base my marketing decisions on comes from data and from listening to the customers. It's all well and good to read about your blogs and see what everybody else is doing, and you have to do that, but at the end of the day you really have to listen to your customer and how your customer is interacting with your product in order to know how best to get more customers like them." –Lorien, PetHub

Companies everywhere are looking for ways to fake this one. Big corporations are paying bots to scan and respond to social media messages. Of course, we've all heard the various naughty companies literally listening to users via televisions, phones, and more. THAT is not what I'm talking about here. Just like any relationship, if you're going to form a bond of any kind with your customers, you need to listen to them. You need to engage with them. You cannot ignore them and expect them to keep coming 'round for a chat and a purchase!

1. Respect them
2. Let them co-create

1. Respect

Building relationships starts with R-E-S-P-E-C-T. Find out what it means to your customer! Here's a few starting points: Don't bombard them, protect their privacy, don't text when they want an email, and take their feedback on board:

- o   81% of U.S. consumers feel loyal to brands that are there when they need them, but otherwise, respect their time and leave them alone.
- o   85% of U.S. consumers are loyal to brands that safeguard and protect the privacy of their personal information.
- o   51% of U.S. consumers are loyal to brands that interact with them through their preferred channels of communication.
- o   97% of consumers said they are somewhat likely to become more loyal to a company that implements their feedback.[29]

2. Let Them Co-Create

"The personalization has gone from three different assortments which were small, medium, and large dog to, I think in January we'll send probably about 140 different assortments: Some dogs like more toys than treats and vice-versa. Some have allergies, some love to destroy plush toys and want really durable things that stand up. As we get more and more information, we feed that back in and try to get the perfect set of products to your dog every month." – Matt, BarkBox

---

"We make a point to really involve our customers in big decisions. We've leveraged consumer feedback for new recipe creation on a number of occasions where we've basically said, 'We are going to create a fish diet and it's going to be grain free. What types of ingredients would you love to see in it? What would you hope we exclude from a particular formulation?' Obviously, we can't please everybody and certainly not all the time, but we can take consensus and say 'Well, the majority of people didn't want flax seed or they did want sweet potatoes but not white potatoes,' or whatever it might be. We can and then go back to them and say, 'Look, we've listened to you and this is what we've created.'"
– Lucy, Honest Kitchen

"Ruffwear products have really been driven by customer needs. People coming to us saying, 'Hey, I've got this problem. How would you solve it?' Coming up with these solutions is really fun. After a year or so, we had different people coming to us saying, 'You know, the big bowl is great, but when we're out hiking, we don't need something so large. Can you make something smaller?' So, we made something smaller, and that suited people's needs. The dealers and retailers bought those... consumers bought those. Then the big bowl was too big, and the little bowl was too small...
'Is there something in between?' and so we came up with a mid-size bowl, and that kind of rounded out our small, medium, and large bowls that we offer today.

I had this dealer in Colorado who asked me one day, 'Have you ever thought about making dog boots?' And I said, 'Why would we make dog boots?' 'I'm looking at this Cabela's magazine right now and there are six different offerings in here. Everything from an Australian lace up leather dog boot to these technical boots that have suspenders.' She said, 'Well that's great, but none of them work.' I asked, 'Well, why don't they work?' She said, 'Well, none of them stay on.' So, I looked at them and I realized that the boots were really long, they went up quite high, they were like a thigh boot on a human. So, I made some mock-ups using fabrics that were proven and tested in outdoor elements and environment, made a couple of boots, and tested them out. You know what, they worked! They stayed on. I wasn't really a believer in boots. I thought they were fou-fou items but I was amazed when I realized the boots really did make a difference in keeping my dog's paws from getting bruised. They actually do allow the dogs to extend their range and continue to be performers when a lot is being asked of them. That is part of the epiphany: from thinking boots are just dress-up items, to really seeing the benefits and then seeing the opportunities for creating several specific boots based on customer needs."
– Patrick, Ruffwear

"The second time we redesigned the site, we looked at all of our competitors and everyone else in the pet space. We were like, 'Okay this is what people like, this is clearly what people resonate with,' and we designed our site to match, but my gut was telling me, 'This is not us.' I asked our designer, 'Just for grins and giggles, would you do a mock-up that looks kinda like this?'
And I told him what I wanted and he did. We put both side by side out in a survey to our users and then we got some random people to do a focus group. 80% of them were drawn towards what my gut was telling me based on who our customers were, and did not like the standard what was prevalent in the pet industry at that time."
– Lorien, PetHub

"Our customers love to talk to us and love to give us feedback and we answer each and every one of them, every single day no matter what, that's what we do. In 2004, we opened up a company store here in Portland, Maine, our home town. We wanted to get in front of the customer and hear direct feedback about all of our products so that we can say, 'Oh, that doesn't work? Oh, we should really change that design,' or 'What are we missing?' or 'What does your dog need?' and it's been phenomenal and it's helped us become so much better and more effective designers and developers of products for dogs." – Stephanie, Planet Dog

Part of listening and implementing your customers' feedback is letting them impact the course of your brand, product strategy, and marketing. After all, if they will tell you want they want, you don't have to spend all that time trying to figure it out with trial-and-error tactics!

Asking your customers with help designing products and allowing them ways to customize them are two core elements of co-creation and they WORK:

- o   44% of U.S. consumers are loyal to brands that actively engage them to help design or co-create products or services.
- o   41% of U.S. consumers are loyal to brands that offer them the opportunity to personalize products to create something that is bespoke to them.[30]

Plus, once a customer has seen proof that you did actually listen, they are officially engaged. Which is a VALUABLE thing for them to be:

---

30 http://blog.accessdevelopment.com/index.php/2013/11/the-ultimate-collection-of-loyalty-statistics

"Engaged consumers buy 90% more frequently, spend 60% more per transaction and are five times more likely to indicate it is the only brand they would purchase in the future. All of these factors lead to engaged customers delivering three times the value to the brand over the course of a year."[31]

3. Build a Brand-Based Culture

"The word I usually use for our culture is inappropriate. Dogs are messy and they're silly and they're playful and they're funny and emotional and passionate. They're all these great words and I think that we try to address them that way and show them that way. I think when you've seen them in the past, you've seen them in advertisements, commercials, out in the world, and they're like perfectly groomed and sitting nicely, coming when called and going straight to the bowl and eating food properly and not spilling it over the floor like my dog does. That's a great dog, and it would be nice to have one of those, but most of them aren't like that. And so I think we want to celebrate who they really are and embrace that."
– Matt, BarkBox

"I am a customer and almost 100% of our employees are customers. We have a work force of, I think it's up to 48 people now, and almost everybody has a pet. We are all super passionate. We have kind of a foodie culture and a passion for pet health and wellbeing."
– Lucy, Honest Kitchen

---

[31] http://blog.accessdevelopment.com/index.php/2013/11/the-ultimate-collection-of-loyalty-statistics

"We've put together a few documents that we use to help guide us, but most of our longer employees are 15-year-plus and so it's pretty engrained in what we are. We don't have to go back to any documents to verify if that kind of scenario. We know in our gut." – Patrick, Ruffwear

"We have a team of amazing, wonderfully passionate dog-loving, brilliant, so smart (way smarter than me) people who work here who are constantly making sure that everything we do achieves at least one of our five core values." – Stephanie, Planet Dog

The culture of your company is a huge contributor to the taste left in a customers' mouth after they interact with your brand. As you grow, your customers' experience and your brand legacy (and in many ways your personal legacy if you're emotionally connected to this brand of yours) is left in the hands of people who are not you. Unfortunately, you will not really get to make a checklist to dictate the culture of your company, and simply allowing staff to bring their dogs to the office or declaring Friday Work From Home Day does not a great culture make.

The energy and productivity that flows through your business, and consequently the experience that your customers have, will be a direct consequence of the attitudes and actions of you and other team members. The company culture you create (intentionally or otherwise) becomes the brand you are.

To start, just like with your customers, the clearer and more soluble your "why" is, the more contagious it will be. The more clear and contagious your why becomes, the easier it will be to identify team members and contractors who are living and breathing embodiments of what you believe.

The more you surround your brand with people who believe in your why, the more likely it will be that the culture that follows will be one that is productive, that you're proud of, and one that top talent will be attracted to. Best of all, people will be working not just for money, but because they believe in the cause. There's no better team than that.

Obviously, ensuring that any staff member who comes in contact with your customers is extensively trained and well-versed in service levels you're proud of (see #4, Surprise and Delight) is a critical part of this culture in action. They need to be able to tell your brand story with as much conviction as you; they need to anticipate the needs of individual customers and respond appropriately and they need to feel like a valuable contributor to the greater "why" you're trying to achieve.

4. Surprise and Delight

After you've ticked all the other boxes (ESPECIALLY getting the "easy to do business with" part of Sense 5), it is time to delegate some resources to surprise and delighting your customers. This is the step beyond being easy. This is the post-purchase manifestation of being the fox pee: pure pleasure. This tool is all about exceeding your customers' expectations: 50% surprise and 50% delight, this practice is meant to truly make your customer feel special.
To implement surprise and delight, you essentially work an extra little something into your process so that at some stage (pre-purchase, at the time of delivery or service, or post-purchase or all of the above) the customer receives some sort surprising and delightful little extra they weren't expecting. It does not have to be expensive to be effective but it does have to both surprise and delight.

"Surprise changes behavior, it's cheap, it turbocharges emotions, and fuels more passionate relationships between customers and brands." - Harvard Business Review[32]

Surprise: Surprise is the wow factor. In order for your efforts to be really noticed, they need to be unanticipated. This is the "wow" or the "how thoughtful" or the "you shouldn't have" feeling you get when you receive something unexpected. Part of the secret here is not to talk about the fact that you do this in your marketing materials or sales page. It needs to remain a surprise! (Although your customers will probably talk about it – boom! Word of mouth!)

Delight: Whatever it is that you deliver, the more relevant and personal it is to the customer the more delight they'll feel. Think of this as the manifestation of the "listening" piece - the delight is proof that you were listening to them, and out of all the customers you help you remembered who they are (or who their pet is) as a unique individual. It also needs to have perceived value and no strings attached, so don't even think about gifting a "$10 off a purchase of $40" kind of thing.

Examples: Handwritten notes, flowers or little gifts, obsessive details: packaging, remembering specific details about their pet, exquisite service: going the extra mile.

Notice I said "work a little something extra into your process." This strategy should be part of your core marketing strategy and naturally integrated into your brand-based culture. Everyone on your team needs to be well-versed in surprising and delighting customers, and ideally, authorized and encouraged to do it spontaneously whenever the opportunity arises!

---

32 https://hbr.org/2013/05/surprise-is-still-the-most-powerful

HINT: Remember a Million Dollar Dog Brand is a Sensational Product meets a Sensational Brand. This is how that SENSATIONAL shows up in your customer's experience!

5. Build Relationships with Partners and Influencers

"We've had some great partnerships. After a few years of producing our boots, we were able to get Vibram (a very popular outsole) on board. They've got great name recognition and respect. For them to come on board with this little dog company really showed me that we were on to something, and people were believing in what we were doing." – Patrick, Ruffwear

"We were fortunate enough early on to partner with L.L. Bean. They make these amazing Bean boots which have this great molded sole. In 1999, we met them because they wanted to sell our products and we said no over and over again because we just knew that we would not be the best partner to them if we tried to sell to them too early on. But they introduced us to this process called molding. Two years later, Orbee-Tuff was introduced and that's what really put us on the map. Orbee balls, I believe, people still know today and think are one of the best products out there." – Stephanie, Planet Dog

"We've done partnerships with big companies, fashion labels, start-ups: We co-brand. All the celebrities, the TV celebrities, the soap opera celebrities wear our stuff, it is really everywhere. Online we have a big group of global brand ambassadors, more specifically on Instagram. They've been very strong in terms of driving sales and driving awareness to the brand. They are called The Zee.Dog Mafia." – Thad, Zee.Dog

"I have this sort of tendency of cold emailing people when I just believe in something. I have a car in Brazil but my girlfriend doesn't and taxi drivers just hate to pick up dogs. It will take about an hour for one to agree to take the dog and he has to be on your lap. So it's always been a hassle for her to get the dog to the beach. One day she called me crying, I was actually here in New York and she was at the beach and she had spent three hours in the hot sun trying to get a cab to go home, and she just couldn't. I started realizing that like her, there were thousands and thousands of people around the world that have the same problem. Just going up and down with taxi drivers who don't want to take their dogs. I've been a fan of Uber for a long time. I use Uber a lot. I started realizing that here was an opportunity for a company that's been disrupting everything that comes in its way, but they weren't really paying attention to one small detail. What about those people that have dogs?

So I literally cold emailed them – and I think the tagline of the email was 'Dogs deserve to ride in comfort too' or something like that. It caught their attention. In the email, I said, 'Listen, I have a very strong brand here in Brazil and I think that I can get a lot of these people who maybe don't know that they can use Uber. This is an opportunity for you guys to get new customers and to get even bigger brand awareness than you already have, and at the end of the day you do something good.

They loved the idea. Basically, you open the Uber app, and instead of Uber X or Uber Black, you have Uber Pet. You press the button and the car that picks you up has seat protectors. Zee.Dog made the seat protectors and the driver gives you a discount code to buy more stuff on the Zee.Dog online store. So it was one of those partnerships where it happened quick, but when it did, people went nuts in Brazil. It was just everywhere. In every single blog, every single TV channel – it was just insane. Again, it was one of those things where we weren't worried about money; we weren't really thinking about product, we were just trying to make people and dogs have a better life and to have more fun. It used to be, 'If I go to the beach I'm going to have trouble getting a cab on the way back.' Now it's not. Literally I can go anywhere now because I have a car that I know is going to pick me and my dog up and the driver is going to pet him and give him some water and a treat, and the seat is going to be protected so I don't have to worry about that. It was simple, but it was huge" – Thad, Zee.Dog

"We work with influencers, you know, breeders, dog trainers, doggie daycare, massage therapists, canine and feline chiropractors and acupuncturists, and all of those types of people who are influencers in some capacity, making sure that they're familiar with our brand, oftentimes providing them with an allowance of product for their own pets in exchange for them kind of chatting to people about it and sowing the seed." – Lucy, Honest Kitchen

Some of the greatest wins in your business are likely to come by pooling your resources with other like-minded brands or leveraging partners with influence. We really are better together, and if you live the Dogly Principles and approach these collaborations generously, even your most direct competitor can become an ally. The sweet spot for partnership is to seek out brands who have the same customer but sell a product or service that is complementary to your own.

Here's a few ways to turn collaboration into win-win relationship-building situations:

- o   Paid influencer content**
- o   Social media 'takeover'
- o   Contests / giveaways with shared prize
- o   Content contributions / interviews
- o   Cross-promoting content / campaigns via email or social media
- o   Bundling brands together in retail display
- o   Co-hosting events
- o   Co-creating products
- o   Sharing the cost for marketing space (ads, booths)
- o   Masterminding (connect on a regular basis to problem solve together)
- o   Sharing speaking / presenting gigs

Just remember when you're reaching out to a competitor or potential partner, always lead with what you have to offer; what you want to give, and not what you want to take!

**Want to find out more about becoming or working with an influencer? We did a fantastic month of content on this subject recently. It's waiting for you at workingwithdog.com/pet-influencers/.

19. That's a Wrap

You did it! You've made it to the end of the book. You've learned about and survived each and every one of the Six Marketing Senses:

1. **Sense of Self:** Why (mission)
2. **Sense of Sight:** Who (audience)
3. **Sense of Hearing:** What (products)
4. **Sense of Touch:** Where (touchpoints)
5. **Sense of Smell:** How 1 (pre-purchase)
6. **Sense of Taste:** How 2 (post-purchase)

You now have the exact roadmap you need – and trust me, you'll need to come back to it again and again, this is not a one-time process! – to build your Million Dollar Dog Brand.

Each of the Six Marketing Stages is made up of some absolutely critical skills that brands become experts in and many businesses don't bother with. Why? Well some of them are difficult to measure, most of them take time to master, and none of them are obvious to most entrepreneurs when they're starting out. Sometimes it may feel like as a brand having to consider all these senses and skills, that you have a harder road towards success than a business.

Many of our Million Dollar Dog Brands mentioned "making life hard for themselves" by obsessing over their Six Marketing Senses. But rest assured, that obsession, that attention and care, that relentless pursuit of showing up as a human who cares rather than a business robot who is only concerned with numero uno, is what will make you nearly impossible to compete with. In marketing textbooks, you'll see this described as a "sustainable competitive advantage," and it's the holy grail of any business. Of course, we call it the Advantage Cycle, and it's the result of building a Million Dollar Dog Brand.Follow this Million Dollar Dog Brand formula and your advantage won't just be sustainable... it won't just give you an edge over your competition... it will change your entire life in ways you can't even fathom. It will turn your business into a brand, your products into a movement and your stress into freedom: Freedom from feeling like a failure or an imposter, financial freedom, lifestyle freedom... freedom to change the world in ways that matter to you.

This formula is so much more than a brand-building tool. For entrepreneurs like you, it's a life changing tool. It's a clarity-creating, time-managing, joy-making, life-saving plan.

Take yourself from wherever you are right now to the life you dream of. It is not an easy path... you may scream, cry, throw things, feel lost, feel found and then feel lost again... you might "know it" before you "feel it" and wonder if you're getting it right at all, but then, maybe one glorious sunny Tuesday, something is going to shift. Click. Settle into place... and you're just going to know, not wonder, but know deep down, exactly what you have to do and from that moment, that glorious, goosebump-covered, lightning-bolt moment, nothing can stop you. You will have finally stepped into your role as the founder of the next Million Dollar Dog Brand, and the world had better take notice, because it will never be the same.

20. Afterword

If you've finished this book and you are both exhilarated and totally overwhelmed, like you're standing at Everest basecamp and you have NO idea how to get up that summit, or why you ever thought it was a good idea to try... fear not. You're not alone.

We can be your Sherpas up the Million Dollar Dog Brand Mountain. The process I've described in this book, as I've warned repeatedly, is not easy. I don't say that over and over to scare you, but to prepare you. I want you to embark upon this journey with open eyes, an open heart, and a full pack, but you do not have to carry it or climb alone!

My entire life's work has led me to this moment: providing resources like this book to help you get to the summit of Million Dollar Dog Brand Mountain faster and with less injury than those who've gone before you. This is my soul's passion - helping petpreneurs like you find your true zone of genius and building a wildly profitable, personally fulfilling brand that makes the lives of animals and the world at large better.

My team and I are all in. Here's how we can help:

JOIN THE GROUP: Working with Dog

Join our brand-building community exclusively for petpreneurs. Our awesome membership spans the globe and together, we are supporting each other while we build our Million Dollar Dog Brands. A mix of exclusive content, access to experts, community support and weekly & monthly Q+A with me makes this space really priceless. I am proud to say we have almost all the same members as when the site launched, which means we must be doing something right! workingwithdog.com/join.

GET ME ALL TO YOURSELF: Million Dollar Dog Brand Formula

I work one-on-one with a very small number of petpreneurs to help them build their Million Dollar Dog Brands. It doesn't matter if you have an existing business that you want to take to the next level, or you just have the glimmer of an idea. I can help you find and develop your why and transform it into something you can see and touch and more importantly, something that your customers will line up to buy! Here's how:

-JUST STRATEGY-

1. Single-topic Intensive: A quick two-hour session to discuss one topic like product strategy, pricing, your why, etc., with a 30-minute follow-up two weeks later. I can accomplish a lot in 15 minutes; you wouldn't believe what we can accomplish in two hours!

2. Million Dollar Dog Brand Formula: My signature 12-week program to build your Million Dollar Dog Brand. We start with a three-hour Kickstarter call to set our three objectives and then we have a call every two weeks for 12 weeks. Most of my MDDB get so much out of this program they sign-up again for another 12 weeks!

- STRATEGY AND DESIGN -

1. Basic Branding: Single-topic intensive and your very own Million Dollar Dog Brand logo identity package plus extra tasty goodies.

2. Million Dollar Dog Brand Starter Kit: Everything above plus the full 12-week Million Dollar Dog Brand Formula program, and you get a few more essential marketing assets to ensure your Marketing Toy Box is full.

3. Million Dollar Dog Brand Expert Kit: Everything above plus a gorgeous, responsive, Wordpress website with extra marketing genius built in. Our entire team contributes to this one, including designers, photographers, copywriters, researchers and analysts.

- MILLION DOLLAR DOG BRAND ONLINE COURSE -

We are in the process of turning our Million Dollar Dog Brand Formula into a comprehensive online course, **coming soon.**

Want to know when it's live? Go let me know at:

workingwithdog.com/million-dollar-dog-brand-camp/

- SPEAKING, PRESENTING or CONTRIBUTING -

If you know of a group, organization, event, or media outlet that would benefit from some of the ideas, strategies, or tools in this book, I have several ways I can deliver them. I love collaborations with like-minded brand builders, and my messages are especially well-suited for startups, female entrepreneurs, and pet industry professionals. Events where I have been invited to speak at include:

- o   Global Pet Expo, US
- o   PATS, UK
- o   Women in the Pet Industry Conference, US
- o   Victoria Stilwell Dog Training Academy, US and UK

Get in touch at hello@workingwithdog.com or visit workingwithdog.com/speaking for a speaking bio and more information.

- BOOKS & RESOURCES -

Here are the books I mentioned in the book, plus a few more essential reads I highly recommend:

Big Magic | Elizabeth Gilbert

Purple Cow | Seth Godin

Emotional Design | Don Norman

You can find more of our book recommendations at: workingwithdog.com/books-recommend/

21. About the Author

J. Nichole Smith is a marketing consultant and branding expert.

In 2005, she founded dane + dane studios, a creative agency for pet businesses. In 2007, she co-founded Dog is Good, a lifestyle company for dog lovers, now a Million Dollar Dog Brand. In 2015, Pet Age Magazine named Nic one of their "40 under 40."

In addition to championing her own brands, Nichole has spent the last decade crafting identities, creative strategies and campaigns for the most influential individuals, media outlets, and brands in the pet industry, including Purina, Petco, and Victoria Stilwell.

In 2012 Nichole's first book Puppyhood was released to critical acclaim. At the same time she traded sunny California for swinging London. In 2014, Nichole graduated with Distinction from Kingston University's MA Marketing program. Immediately afterward, she opened Little and Large, a fine-art pet photography studio and dog boutique in SW London.

In 2016, Nichole sold her retail business and launched Working with Dog, a community to help petpreneurs find freedom by building brands. Nichole also offers luxury business retreats for petpreneurs, one-to-one consulting programs and keynote speeches on topics relating to brand building and entrepreneurship. She is also proud to be on the faculty of the Victoria Stilwell Dog Training Academy.

Nic's home is in London but you'll often find her traveling around Europe with her husband and their more-baby-than-dog, Charleston (#bromancesupreme). Join them on their adventures on Instagram: @workingwithdog

27808589R00140

Printed in Great Britain
by Amazon